BIBLICAL
FOUNDATIONS
for the
CELL-BASED
CHURCH

New Testament Insights for the
Twenty-First Century Church

JOEL COMISKEY, PH.D.

www.joelcomiskeygroup.com

Published by CCS Publishing
23890 Brittlebush Circle
Moreno Valley, CA 92557 USA
1-888-344-CELL

Cover design and Layout by Sarah Comiskey
Editing by Scott Boren

LCCN: 2012900752
ISBN:978-0-9843110-3-3

CCS Publishing is the book-publishing division of Joel Comiskey Group, a resource and coaching ministry dedicated to equipping leaders for cell-based ministry.

Find us on the World Wide Web at **www.joelcomiskeygroup.com**

PRAISES FOR
Biblical Foundations for the Cell-Based Church

"Joel Comiskey effectively draws upon the skills of a careful interpreter, the heart of a pastor, and a background in cross-cultural missions to craft this thoughtful and informative treatment of cell-group ministry. An attentive reading of Biblical Foundations for the Cell-Based Church will challenge—in the most positive sense of the word— traditional church models and approaches to ministry driven by consumer-oriented pragmatism. I warmly commend Joel's book to pastors and others who long to enjoy the kind of relationships experienced by the early Christians, and who wish to base their understanding of community on the theological bedrock of biblical truth."

—**Joe Hellerman, Ph.D.,** Professor of NT Language and Literature, Talbot School of Theology, Team Pastor at Oceanside Christian Fellowship

"Just when it seems that everything has been written that could be said about the church, its nature and its expansion, when all the cliched formulas have been reshuffled ad infinitum, all the accusations dispensed and the mea culpas chanted, suddenly appears a book that can be ignored only to the Kingdom's detriment. This passionate appeal for the rediscovery of the dynamic of the early church that conquered the pagan world within a couple of centuries begins with an unimpeachable Trinitarian theological grounding for the definition of the church. It continues with a careful consideration of the historical and cultural factors that contributed to the shaping of its life and worship, and it culminates with pertinent advice for the transposition of the author's findings to the contemporary church scene. Required reading for pastors and other leaders of static, moribund and/or dysfunctional congregations."

—**Gilbert Bilezikian,** Professor emeritus, Wheaton College, Willow Creek Community Church

"Dr. Comiskey does us a great service in shining a spotlight on both the form and function of the early church of the New Testament era. This book will challenge anyone serious about God's work to do it more biblically and, therefore, more effectively. The errors of "pragmatism", "personal preference", and even "biblical blueprint-ism" will surely find a refreshing biblical remedy for the nature of the New Testament church in these pages."

—**Rad Zdero, PhD,** author of *The Global House Church Movement* and *Letters to the House Church Movement.*

"In the first part of this book, Joel Comiskey takes the reader deep into the nature of God as the foundation of the theology of the Early Church. Then, he gives us insights into how to live out that amazing theology in the great mystery of Trinitarian community."

—**Bill Beckham,** author of *The Second Reformation*

"This book is a biblical, theological, and practical study of families, households, and house/cell churches in the New Testament. Although the author does not believe "that God gave an exact prescriptive pattern in the New Testament called cell-church," he identifies a number of enduring values in these entities such as hospitality, discipline, leadership and mutual accountability that could strengthen the church today and justify the implementation of a cell-based ministry. This book is to be commended for avoiding a pragmatic ("how") and dogmatic ("God's design") approach by focusing on the "why" and challenging the contemporary church to consider such a model."

—**Arthur G. Patzia, PhD,** Senior Professor of New Testament, Fuller Theological Seminary and author of *The Emergence of the Church*

TABLE OF
CONTENTS

DEDICATION

To Ralph Neighbour,
who has embodied and taught the main truth
of this book "Theology Breeds Methodology"
better than anyone I know.

ACKNOWLEDGMENTS

I'm the author of this book, but I've had plenty of help along the way. In the long process to make this book a reality, many hands and eyes have handled and contributed to the final work. Several people deserve special recognition.

Special thanks to Brian McLemore, World Bible Translation Center's (www.wbtc.org) Vice President of Translations, who once again critiqued my efforts, and the result is a better book.

Anne White saved me a lot of grief by checking the grammatical details of the book (e.g., footnotes, capitalization, etc.) as well as challenging the logic of certain statements. Anne has been a friend since my 1996 Fuller days, and I greatly appreciate her expert advice.

Jay Stanwood, a retired engineer and good friend of mine for about thirty-five years, offered key suggestions that made this book a lot better.

I'm grateful to Rad Zdero, author and researcher on house churches, for giving me valuable recommendations. He made key suggestions that I readily added to this book.

Bill Joukhadar, a small group expert living in Australia, made a special effort to look at this book and offered advice on the biblical references.

My good friends and team members on the JCG board, Rob Campbell and Steve Cordle, both encouraged and challenged my writing. I really appreciated the time they took to look over this book.

Scott Boren, my chief editor, made wide-ranging suggestions to shape this book. I asked Scott to rewrite Chapter 1 and Chapter 9, and this current book is much better as a result of his help. Scott and I have worked together on twenty-one of my twenty-five books.

Lastly, I want to thank my wonderful wife, Celyce, for being my best friend and providing the liberty and encouragement to write this book.

INTRODUCTION

Most small group books on the market are pragmatic. They talk about how to make cell groups work, so your church will grow, become healthier, or both. This book is different. The purpose is to answer the *why* question. Why cell ministry? Or put another way, What does the Bible say about small group involvement in the church?

Initially I researched cell churches looking for pragmatic answers to help churches grow. I wanted to discover the causes of group multiplication and church growth, so I looked for clues in eight different contexts and cultures, discovered principles, categorized them, and then communicated those findings to the worldwide cell church.

I wrote books about those principles for many years, but I slowly began to see the need for a better foundation for small group ministry. I became increasingly aware of the need to base cell ministry on the Bible rather than pragmatism.

The goal of this book, therefore, is to discover the biblical underpinnings for small group ministry. Because the purpose is to uncover biblical principles, I won't be writing about modern day cell church ministry. Apart from my first chapter on discovering a biblical foundation for the cell-based church, I have avoided talking about modern day models, whether it be cell church, house church, or small group ministry.

Normally when starting a book, I present clear-cut definitions in the introduction. In this book, I have chosen to allow the Bible to speak for itself and present its own definition of how the early church functioned, and then to allow the biblical evidence to critique or promote modern day cell-based ministry. My goal is to get inside the worldview of the church of the first century and allow that experience to shape how we do church today.

I will reference writings of biblical scholars and historians of the first century church to discover what the context, culture, and household environment was like back then. I draw heavily from Roger Gehring's work, *House Church and Mission* and scholars such as Arthur G. Patzia, Carolyn Osiek, Leo G. Perdue, Gerhard Lohfink, Ritva H. Williams, Rodney Stark, and Stanley J. Grenz. These researchers, along with many others, helped me understand the biblical worldview.

In the first section, I'll cover foundational biblical principles for small group ministry. I'll discuss biblical hermeneutics,[1] the character of God, family imagery, and Christ's focus on earth.

Chapter 1 explores how people often read themes into the Bible to justify their own point of view. The cell church movement has done the same thing, and I'm as guilty as anyone. The point of this chapter is to return to a biblical hermeneutic that allows the Bible to speak for itself.

The subject of Chapter 2 is how small group ministry flows from God himself. God is a Trinity. He is one, but exists in

---

1 Hermeneutics is the study of methodological principles for arriving at a correct interpretation of Scripture.

three persons. Within the Godhead, perfect unity exists. Because God's nature is communal, small group ministry must be based on God's character. I show how God is working in believers to bring about this relational change.

Chapter 3 establishes the family emphasis in Genesis, and how families journeyed in households throughout the Old Testament. God chose Abraham and his family line to bless the nations. Jesus focused on a new family comprised of his followers. The early church continued this family emphasis, using the homes of believers to highlight this new relationship. My research, in fact, points out that family is the principal image for the New Testament church. This imagery flows naturally from the house church background.

In Chapter 4, we'll see how Jesus came to establish God's kingdom. He ministered with his twelve for three years, preparing them to be the leaders of the early church. Jesus chose the home as the base for his own operations, and then sent his disciples out two by two to penetrate the homes of unbelievers.

The second section probes deeply into New Testament history to discern how God used the home to transform the Mediterranean world. This section covers different aspects of the early house church, the role of the ancient *oikos*,[2] leadership development, and the relationship between house churches.

Chapter 5 examines how house churches were key to the expansion of early Christianity. The house church environment accentuated the bonds of family life and demonstrated God's love to neighbors and extended family. In this chapter, we will explore the house church context, size, and content of house meetings.

The theme of Chapter 6 is how the early church evangelized from house-to-house. This chapter goes into detail about

---

2 *Oikos* is the Greek word for household, extended family, or social circle.

ancient *oikos* relationships—the extended family networks of early church culture. God used these extended family relationships to penetrate the Mediterranean world. Early apostles, like Paul, planted house churches that eventually transformed the Roman Empire. The genius of the movement was the transformation of *oikos* relationships through house-to-house ministry.

Chapter 7 explains how early church leadership flowed naturally from the house ministry. New leaders—often the hosts of the house churches—came out of the house structure and eventually wore the title of elder, pastor, or overseer. God used men and women through their God-given spiritual gifts to lead the early church. They practiced the priesthood of all believers in the house church context, and God developed leadership through that environment.

In Chapter 8 we'll see how the New Testament writers used *ecclesia*[3] to refer to both large and small group gatherings. In Jerusalem and Corinth, house churches gathered regularly to worship. Although house churches in other parts of the Mediterranean world were connected through apostolic leadership, the larger group gatherings were less frequent and more spontaneous.

The third section is Chapter 9. It summarizes previous chapters and then applies the principles to the twenty-first century church. It's not enough to reflect on biblical principles and the context of the New Testament church. We need to understand how those biblical principles transform ministry and apply them to today's church. In this chapter we'll look at ways pastors and cell leaders can apply biblical principles.

---

3 *Ecclesia* is the Greek word for a "gathering of people." Early Christians adopted this term to refer to their Christian gatherings. The word ecclesia is translated "church" in English versions of the Bible.

Part 1

ESTABLISHING A STRONG FOUNDATION

Chapter One
FOUNDATIONS:
SAND OR ROCK?

Why develop cell ministry in a local church? Why are cell groups so important to what God is doing around the world today? What's the foundation for small group ministry?

These are crucial questions. Over the years, thousands and thousands have tried cell groups. Sadly, many have started on foundations of sand, failing to dig deep enough to build upon the rock. In the mid-1990s, for example, cell groups became a popular fad.

In 1995, Ralph W. Neighbour Jr. returned to the U.S. from Singapore. Over the previous five years, his book *Where Do We Go From Here?* sold over one hundred thousand copies. He provided practical resources to help churches implement a cell-based approach in their churches. And his strategy had seen great success in the church he helped develop in Singapore. He had also created a resource called *The Year of Transition,* which he piloted with hundreds of churches in South Africa.

Carl George also sparked a lot of interest in small group ministry with his 1991 book, *Prepare Your Church for the Future.* George's research was especially important because he contextualized the worldwide cell emphasis to fit a North American reality. Much of George's initial research came from studying Dale Galloway's New Hope Community Church in Portland, Oregon, but George went beyond NHCC to apply small group principles to the North American church in general.

Beyond Neighbour and George, some very large churches and significant denominational leaders embraced the cell-based approach. The cell church had suddenly shifted from an obscure idea to something that prominent seminaries taught about and offered in their degree concentrations.

However, in the Western world, people's fascination with cell-based churches waned. Many moved on to hotter topics. What interests me, however, is how many significant leaders in those early days proclaimed that cell church was not just a program, but the way to do church. Oddly, many of those churches have set aside cell ministry. It's no longer the priority.

We can learn from these examples. When a church does not develop a strong foundation upon which to build cell groups, the reason for doing cell ministry will also shift like sand.

It's the basic "rubber band" effect that comes with the implementation of a new idea. Often people get excited about the potential of cell-based church life. They begin making the change and as they do, they are stretching a rubber band with a finger on their right hand away from an anchored and stable finger on the left. However, when they fail to establish sound foundations for what they are doing, they will experience a pull from the anchored left hand, which represents the traditional ways of doing church. Those traditional ways are in centuries of use, so the pull is strong.

At the same time, I've observed many churches implement cell church ministry. One of the key differences in these churches was establishing a strong foundation for why they were doing cells. These deep convictions carried them through the tough times and caused them to stay firm while waiting for God to bring the results. In other words, they developed their small groups on a solid biblical rock, rather than sand.

COMMON FOUNDATIONS THAT END UP BEING SAND

Jesus says:

Therefore everyone who hears these words of mine and puts them into practice is like a wise man who built his house on the rock. The rain came down, the streams rose, and the winds blew and beat against that house; yet it did not fall, because it had its foundation on the rock. But everyone who hears these words of mine and does not put them into practice is like a foolish man who built his house on sand. The rain came down, the streams rose, and the winds blew and beat against that house, and it fell with a great crash (Matthew 7:24-27).

If you base cell ministry upon shifting sand, when the rains come, the streams rise, and the winds blow, you will return to what is familiar. It's human nature to go back to what you know to survive as a church. What I have observed over the years, however, is that these weak foundations of sand have become the main reasons for implementing cell ministry. Here are a few shallow foundations:

Church Growth

My PhD is in intercultural studies; practically, however, it's a PhD in church growth studies. My academic mentor was Peter Wagner, the student of Donald McGavran, who became the marquee name synonymous with church growth theory during the 1980s and 1990s.

Although I embraced church growth in the early years as the key reason for doing cell church ministry, I've since come to view church growth as a foundation of sand.

When I first started studying cell ministry, I became enamored with its potential for church growth, but I didn't prioritize the theological side of cell ministry as much as the pragmatic aspect.

My first book, *Home Cell Group Explosion*, focused on the rapid multiplication and evangelism of cells, and then my second book, *Reap the Harvest*, emphasized the growth of cell churches based on common principles. At that time, I was a missionary in Ecuador, and our cell church was seeing amazing church growth. I believed certain leaders in the cell movement were not pragmatic enough. I wanted to show the world that cell church had to work for it to have relevance.

In June 1998, I toured five major U.S. cities for *Touch Publications*, my book publisher. My seminar topic was cell church. Most of the pastors who attended were struggling. They simply were not experiencing the rapid church growth I highlighted in my books. Most of them talked about their long, long transition and the difficulties of cell ministry.

As I showed them PowerPoint photos of growing cell churches, they were impressed by the church growth examples, but were generally discouraged by their own lack of growth. I thought they were doing something wrong. *They just don't understand how to make cell church work. I will show them.* I returned to Ecuador, critical of the North American church.

A few years later, I took another trip to the U.S. and met with a denominational superintendent who had developed material for transitioning churches. His strategy called for a long, slow process. I criticized his approach, thinking he really didn't know how to establish a growing church. He looked directly at me and said, "Joel, you don't understand ministry in North America. It's tough and completely different from what you are used to."

He turned out to be right.

I moved to North America in 2001 from Ecuador. I jumped right into the battle , coaching pastors, doing seminars, and even planted a cell church with another pastor. I intended to find the keys that would unlock a cell church explosion in the United States and the Western world.

Church growth was much slower in the West. I could "grow a church" more quickly by not emphasizing cell ministry! Some people told us they were looking for a church in which they wouldn't be known. One Christian said to me, "I need a church where I don't have to do much." Very few were interested in the additional commitments of cell ministry. Some churches were "growing" by not requiring much of their members and allowing them to remain anonymous.

Church growth was slow in North America because spiritual revival was missing. Many didn't have time to join a group and were not interested in close and personal community, going through an equipping track, practicing relational evangelism, and participating in a planned multiplication.

Over time, I became convinced that cell church was more of a purification or transformation strategy for the church in North America. Over a long period of time, I began to see cell ministry as much more than a technique of church growth. I realized that my former church growth theology was deficient.

I came to understand that biblical truth is the final judge of church growth or any other philosophy of ministry.

I made a decision to base my life and ministry on Scripture, and the pieces of the puzzle began to fall into place. I found myself pleasantly surprised with how well the cell church strategy meshed with biblical theology. I came to believe that the key reason we do cell church is because of theological convictions, and that those biblical convictions should never be secondary, but rather, they should be the primary reason.

Theology gives wings to cell ministry because it provides the basis for implementation in both receptive and non-receptive areas. Following the cell church strategy does not result in instant church growth. It takes time to change traditional thinking, develop the lay people to do the work of the ministry, and engage in relational evangelism. Some churches might even lose members in early stages of the process.

Cell church principles and practices must be built on a biblical foundation if churches are to become healthier and make more and better disciples. It's not a quick growth strategy, but rather, a biblical one. Cell groups provide the environment to form disciples. In certain receptive areas around the world, multiplication happens rapidly because people are coming to Christ, being trained, and starting new cells. In more resistant areas around the world, however, the process takes much longer because the soil is harder. No matter where the church is established, it must depend on biblical truth rather than outward results.

Church Health

In the early 2000s, church health became a hot topic. Pollsters like George Barna, professors like Peter Wagner, and pastors like Elmer Towns produced lists of characteristics that described healthy churches. Rick Warren in *The Purpose-Driven Church*, says, "The key issue for churches in the twenty-first century will be church health, not church growth."[4]

The most definitive guide on church health is *Natural Church Development*.[5] After performing extensive statistical research on tens of thousands of churches around the world, Christian Schwarz and his team determined that there are eight quality characteristics of healthy churches. They include:

- Empowering leadership
- Gift-oriented ministry
- Passionate spirituality
- Functional structures
- Inspiring worship services
- Holistic small groups
- Need-oriented evangelism
- Loving relationships

Schwarz went even further by saying, "If we were to identify any one principle as the 'most important'—even though our research shows that the interplay of all basic elements is important—then without a doubt it would be the multiplication of small groups."[6]

Many read this and saw cell groups as the answer to having a healthy church. Since the publication of *Natural Church Development*, further research has shown that cell-based churches

---

4 Rick Warren, *The Purpose-Driven Church*: Growing without Compromising Your Message and Mission (Grand Rapids, MI: Zondervan, 1995), p. 17.
5 Christian Schwarz, *Natural Church Development* (Carol Stream, IL: Church Smart Resources, 1996).
6 Ibid., p. 33.

are statistically healthier in all eight categories than those that are not cell-based.[7]

These statistics are encouraging, but are they enough to sustain a small group ministry over time? Do they provide the strong foundational rails necessary to press on in cell church ministry when obstacles occur, church growth doesn't happen, and a new, easier method presents itself? Schwarz's research might be a motivation to start cell ministry, but can the church health argument sustain it over time?

Spiritual Revelation

Some pastors developed cell church ministry because of a spiritual encounter with God. Larry Stockstill, for example, wrote about his encounter in the opening chapter of his book *The Cell Church*.[8] He sensed God telling him that two things were coming to America: harvest and hostility, and that the way to prepare for this harvest and hostility was through cells. This experience led him to discover the power of cell groups as a way of dealing with the coming harvest and hostility.

Stockstill's book was a great inspiration to me and provided many valuable insights into Bethany World Prayer Center's journey of becoming a cell church. According to the book, it seems that God's direct word to Bethany was the primary justification for cell group ministry.

Many pastors have heard God directly speaking to them, and for this reason they start their cell church journey. But is this

---

7 A study comparing the Natural Church Development scores of cell churches and non-cell churches showed that cell churches overall scored significantly higher in all areas than non-cell churches. Combined cell church scores averaged 59 while combined non-cell church scores averaged 45. More information on this study can be obtained at: http://www.joelcomiskeygroup.com/articles/churchLeaders/cellChurchStudy.htm

8 Larry Stockstill, *The Cell Church (Ventura,* CA: Regal Books, 1998), p. 13.

enough to sustain them over time? What will happen when the storms come? I do believe that God speaks directly to us today, and we need to constantly be hearing from him, both for direction and renewal of the vision. But again, is spiritual illumination sufficient to continue on the cell church journey?

Everybody Has Small Groups

Robert Wuthnow and George Gallup, Jr. have been instrumental in researching the resurgence of small groups across the United States. They estimate that seventy-five million adults in the United States participate in some kind of small group.[9] These small groups include both church groups (e.g., Bible studies, Sunday school, cell groups) as well as non-church groups (e.g., support groups, recovery groups). One out of six of those seventy-five million people are new members of small groups; thus disclosing that, at least in the United States, the small group movement is alive and well.[10]

Lyle Schaller has noted the explosion of small group interest in the U.S. After listing twenty new innovations in the modern American church Schaller says, ". . . perhaps most important of all, is the decision by tens of millions of teenagers and adults to place a high personal priority on weekly participation in serious, in-depth, lay-led, and continuing Bible study and prayer groups."[11]

Obviously a lot of people are participating in small groups. But is this a strong foundation? Some pastors are not aware of

---

9 Robert Wuthnow, *I Come Away Stronger: How Small Groups Are Shaping American Religion* (Grand Rapids, MI: Eerdmans, 1994), p. 370

10 Ibid., p. 371.

11 Lyle E. Schaller, *The New Reformation: Tomorrow Arrived Yesterday* (Nashville, TN: Abingdon Press, 1995), p. 14.

the biblical values that undergird their philosophy of ministry and end up choosing the most popular strategy at the time. "Of course I'm doing small groups," says the pastor. Yet, if this is the motivation, it's just as easy to quit, as it is to join.

THEOLOGY BREEDS METHODOLOGY

If you want to continue over the long haul, your cell group methodology must rest upon a sure theological foundation. No one understood this better than the primary pioneer of cell church thinking, Ralph Neighbour. He has an entire section in his book *Where Do We Go From Here* entitled "Theology Breeds Methodology." He would always start his cell conferences with a talk on this topic. And Ralph has seen his share of resistance to his core cell convictions. But to this day, even into his eighties, he is still traveling the globe helping to establish cell churches.

Bill Beckham also believes that a church or pastor should never change a structure until changing values. The values Beckham is talking about are biblical ones. Theological values must guide methodology. The biblical foundation must guide all we do and say.

ALMOST BIBLICAL

I believe most of you reading this book may agree with me so far. You might even think that I'm "preaching to the choir." But let me ask: What kind of biblical foundation is the one built upon the rock? You might be surprised that many foundations appear biblical but end up being sand. Let me identify some of these:

Biblical Idealism

By far the most quoted passage used to justify the cell-based approach to church is Acts 2:42-46,

> They devoted themselves to the apostles' teaching and to fellowship, to the breaking of bread and to prayer. Everyone was filled with awe, and many wonders and miraculous signs were done by the apostles. All the believers were together and had everything in common. Selling their possessions and goods, they gave to anyone as he had need. Every day they continued to meet together in the temple courts. They broke bread in their homes and ate together with glad and sincere hearts.

This wonderful text has helped the church understand the connection between cells and celebration[12] in the Jerusalem church. Yet, it's not enough of a biblical foundation to carry a church through the storms of ministry.

Often churches with nostalgia, hopes, and dreams hold up this idea and proclaim something like, "If we just meet in small groups, worship on the weekends, and pray hard, the church will not be able to handle all the baptisms." But after a year or two, nothing really changes, people become disillusioned, and the leaders move on to another idea.

We have to be careful not to erect entire models from a few New Testament passages. I've appreciated my colleague, Brian McLemore, a Bible translator with World Bible Translation Center, who has graciously reviewed many of my books before going to print. Brian consistently challenges my dogmatism and

---

12 When I use the word *celebration* in this book, I'm referring to the large group gathering to worship and hear God's Word. Most celebration services take place on Sunday, but some churches have their large group gatherings on different days of the week.

biased thinking, specifically with regard to extracting an exact cell church model from the pages of Scripture. In reality, the best we can do is to derive principles for cell churches from the Bible.

We must remember that the phrase "cell church" is a technical term for a particular present day application of biblical principles, not an exact practice of the New Testament. The early church never used the term cell church ministry.

We can, however, discern a descriptive pattern of small and large groups. Paul preached publicly and from house-to-house. The early disciples gathered to hear the apostle's teaching publicly, but they also met in homes for fellowship, the Lord's Supper, and spiritual growth.

In all honesty, I don't believe God gave an exact prescriptive pattern in the New Testament called *cell church*. After all, the early church met every day in the temple courts and from house-to-house. If we wanted to talk about a once and for all cell-celebration pattern, should the local church meet every day? Few people would agree with this. It's hard enough to meet in celebration each Sunday.

As we will see in the New Testament, believers met in house churches and at times those house churches celebrated together. In other words, there was a connection between the house churches. Today, modern day cell churches connect the cells into a celebration. Some cell churches are very structured, while other cell churches are simple and connect the cells less frequently.

Often we read the Bible looking for an ideal "magic pill," which will make the church work and grow like it did in those early days. But meeting in houses and in the temple courts does not automatically make everything better.

Proof Texting

Another way to search for a biblical foundation is to look for proof texts that stipulate how we should meet.[13] Of course, the New Testament contains many texts that talk about churches that met in homes:

- Acts 12:12: When this had dawned on him, he went to the house of Mary the mother of John, also called Mark, where many people had gathered and were praying.
- Acts 20:20: You know that I have not hesitated to preach anything that would be helpful to you but have taught you publicly and from house-to-house.
- Romans 16:3-5: Greet Priscilla and Aquila, my fellow workers in Christ Jesus. . . . Greet also the church that meets at their house.
- 1 Corinthians 16:19: The churches in the province of Asia send you greetings. Aquila and Priscilla greet you warmly in the Lord, and so does the church that meets at their house.
- Colossians 4:15: Give my greetings to the brothers at Laodicea, and to Nympha and the church in her house.
- Philemon 2: to Apphia our sister, to Archippus our fellow soldier and to the church that meets in your home.

All the New Testament letters were written to first century house churches. Some people insist that anything that does not follow this pattern of meeting in homes is unbiblical.

---

13 Proof texting is the practice of using isolated Scripture (with no regard for the original content) to support a previously held position.

Although we can say that the early church met in homes, we are unwise to try to build an exact pattern for every modern church. This is what I call *proof texting* because no absolute pattern for house churches exists. We can't copy the exact prescription of frequency or the exact culture of the early church. Roger Gehring says,

> The time span separating the NT from our present situation must be kept in mind, and here again we need to distinguish geographically: the ancient oikos as extended family including slaves, hired laborers, and clients, with its fundamental significance for society and economy, does not exist as such anymore, at least not in the Western world. Our term for family is no longer synonymous with that of the ancient household.[14]

Dennis McCallum, lead pastor of Xenos Christian Fellowship, says, "Scripture never commands us to have our meetings in homes . . ."[15] McCallum goes on to say, "We can marshal some good, common sense arguments suggesting it might be a good idea."[16]

Rather than using proof texts, we have to do the hard work of putting the pieces together and filling in a few gaps to define principles for today's church. The way the early church met was so second nature to them that their writings do not give us much information about how the churches actually functioned.

---

14 Roger W. Gehring, *House Church and Mission: The Importance of Household Structures in Early Christianity* (Peabody, MA: Hendrickson, 2004), p. 301.
15 Dennis McCallum, *Members of One Another* (Columbus, OH: New Paradigm, 2010), p. 119.
16 Ibid., p. 119

Searching for God's Sacred Numbering System

A few years ago, the number twelve became significant in cell church circles. Many church leaders gave the number twelve great theological importance, saying it had a special anointing attached to it. If you could develop twelve leaders, you would reach a place of spiritual blessing. In fact, the International Charismatic Mission in Bogota, Colombia claimed to find special significance for the number twelve throughout the Bible.

If you were to visit the International Charismatic Mission, you'd see banners hanging from the ceiling, proclaiming the number twelve. All cell leaders are looking for their twelve disciples. Pastor Castellanos testifies that the vision of the government of twelve disciples was given to him by the Lord as a direct revelation.[17]

The number twelve is not the only number that carries great weight in the Bible. There were *three* disciples who had special intimacy with Jesus, the resurrection of Jesus took place on the *third* day, and there were *three* crosses at Calvary. God created the heavens and earth in *seven* days and the sabbatical year occurred every *seven* years. The Day of Atonement occurred in the *seventh* month. *Seven* signified fulfillment and perfection. The

---

17 César Castellanos preached that the twelve stones that Elijah used to build Jehovah's sacrifice was the key to God answering his prayer (Claudia & César Castellanos, audio cassette, Como influir en otros [How to Influence Others] January 2002 conference in Bogota). Castellanos says, "The model of the twelve restores the altar of God that is in ruins" (César Castellanos, The Ladder of Success (London: Dovewell Publications, 2001), p. 25). We're told that Elijah would not have chosen Elisha if Elisha would have been plowing with eleven instead of twelve oxen, and that the Holy Spirit at Pentecost came when Matthias had replaced Judas, thus completing the number twelve (Claudia and César Castellanos, The Vision of Multiplication, audio cassette [Bethany World Prayer Center: International Cell Conference, 2001]. César Castellanos and the pastors at ICM will tell you that the vision of the number twelve came directly from God, and therefore we must follow this revelation. They often justify this particular number by referring to a direct revelation from God.

number *ten* signifies completeness, as illustrated in the *Ten* Commandments. *Forty* is associated with God's mighty acts in the history of Israel and the church.

While significance is attached to numbers found in the Bible, the New Testament provides no evidence that the apostles or other church leaders attached any significance to a specific number of disciples chosen in a church. In Acts, the New Testament history book, you won't find the apostles diligently looking for twelve disciples to follow Jesus' pattern of twelve disciples. To apply theological significance to a particular number of disciples in the church today, it would be necessary to find many more examples of this practice in the Bible. I find no reason to idealize the number twelve in Acts or the Epistles. In addition, this idea is absent in church history during two thousand years of theological reflection.

Small Groups as a Secondary Option

Over the years, most church traditions have concluded that since the New Testament does not give us specific instructions about how the church should function, we are left to figure out the best options regarding what works and what does not work in specific cultures.

As a result, most have found it much easier to focus their energies on getting people to attend the weekly large group worship service. When the writer of Hebrews states, "Do not forsake the assembling of yourselves together" (Hebrews 10:25), preachers talk about the importance of attending Sunday services.

Yet, when the writer of Hebrews penned those words, he was not imagining what many think about church, in the modern sense. Many today envision a worship service with a song set, a sermon, and some kind of invitation to respond. Others read from a common prayer book and serve communion at the altar. The writer of Hebrews, however, was thinking about something much more organic, relational, and informal—the house church setting.

Small groups are not new in the church. Small groups are not unique to the cell church or cell-based church structure. Church history reveals that small groups have been crucial to church life for a long time. However, in most cases, small groups have been a secondary option, not the basis of church life. Most leaders elevate the large group as primary and the small group as optional. The New Testament writers were thinking about church much differently than we do today.

A SURE FOUNDATION

How then can we embrace a foundation that serves well through the rain and the wind? Let me state up front that this will require some thinking and reflection. We will have to understand the context in which the Bible was written. We must resist the urge to have our pragmatic questions answered. This will require us to slow down and listen.

During research for this book, many of my preconceived ideas disappeared, and I began to see related patterns and principles throughout the Old and New Testaments. The biblical stories began to mold and shape my thinking. This caused me to go deeper and deeper into the worldview of the New Testament church and then apply it to today's church.

The process was similar to when I first went to Ecuador as a missionary. My wife and I had written academic papers on Latin American culture. Then we lived a year with a Costa Rican family in San Jose, Costa Rica. All the while we were testing and adjusting our theoretical base from the previous research. When we arrived in Ecuador, we made more adjustments, more midcourse corrections, and we eventually began to understand the core Ecuadorian values. After a while, the ways of Ecuadorian life became second nature.

This is how we will develop a sure foundation. In the following chapters, we'll look at the nature of God and then discover how God's nature overflows to his creation and ultimately to the character and function of the church.

Chapter Two

GOD'S TRINITARIAN NATURE

Who is God? What is he like? In Western, individualistic cultures, there's a tendency to define God as an entrepreneurial lone ranger, someone who is just like us. In Eastern cultures, God is often envisioned as having many forms with a multitude of names and reincarnations.

The only way to know God is to find out what he has revealed. Theology, in fact, is the study of God. The word theology is derived from *theos* (God) and *logia* (logic, discourse, or utterance). Theology in its root form is the discussion about God. While we can implicitly see God's power and grandeur in nature, only the Bible explicitly reveals his character and divine being.

The apostle Paul, writing in the context of the idol worshipping culture in Corinth, says,

For even if there are so-called gods, whether in heaven or on earth (as indeed there are many "gods" and many "lords"), yet for us there is but one God, the Father, from whom all things came and for whom we live; and there is but one Lord, Jesus Christ, through whom all things came and through whom we live (1 Corinthians 8:5-6).

Under divine inspiration, Paul and the other writers of Scripture wrote the truth about God's nature. Those leaders who followed them, however, were left the task of categorizing the biblical teaching about God into a unified whole.

The early church fathers were often compelled to do "theology" because of the existence of many false cults defining God according to their own preconceived ideas. The church fathers wrestled with the biblical evidence about God and his character, and the teaching about God's triune nature eventually emerged. Stanley Grenz describes the process,

The process that eventually netted the church's teaching about God as triune was generated by a theological puzzle that lay at the very basis of the Christian community. The early theologians found themselves grappling with a three-part question: how could the confession of the lordship of Jesus and the experience of the indwelling Holy Spirit be understood within the context of the nonnegotiable commitment to the one God that the early believers retained from their connection with Israel?[18]

The triune nature of God describes a God who possesses mutuality within his own being. Rather than promoting an

---

18 Stanley J. Grenz, *The Named God and the Question of Being* (Louisville, KY: Westminster, 2005), p. 293.

individualistic, lone ranger God, the doctrine of the Trinity emphasizes life, love, and movement within the Godhead. Thomas F. Torrance writes,

> While the Lord Jesus Christ constitutes the pivotal center of our knowledge of God, God's distinctive self-revelation as Holy Trinity, One Being, Three Persons, creates the overall framework within which all Christian theology is to be formulated. Understandably, therefore, the doctrine of the Holy Trinity has been called the innermost heart of Christian faith and worship, the central dogma of classical theology, the fundamental grammar of our knowledge of God.[19]

As Torrance points out, the doctrine of the Trinity is foundational to Christianity. It not only defines who we worship and serve, but this doctrine also guides the church to practice love, care, and unity.

WHO IS THE TRINITY?

We see many expressions of the Trinity in Scripture. In Genesis 1:26, for example, God says, "Let us make man in our image, after our likeness." God designates himself as plural. Although God here is not describing his exact image, he is connecting his image to human beings. In other words, God is saying he created humanity to reflect his own relational essence. Stanley Grenz writes,

---

19 Thomas F. Torrance, *The Christian Doctrine of God, One Being Three Persons* (Edinburgh, Scotland: T&T Clark, 1996), p. 2.

Genesis 1:26 opens the way to view the self-reference as indicating a plurality within the divine unity. This, in turn, raises the possibility that creation in the imago dei endows human sexual differentiation with significance as reflecting something about the creator . . . If the "Let us" of Gen. 1:26 points to the presence of a plurality within the one God, then some type of relationality characterizes the Creator. Indeed, this exegetical conclusion finds a hermeneutical confirmation in the subsequent salvation-historical narrative as culminating in the church's doctrine of the Trinity.[20]

Genesis 3:22 says something similar, "The man has now become like one of us, knowing good and evil." Then in Genesis 11:7 we read, "Come, let us go down and confuse their language so they will not understand each other." Isaiah 6:8 says, "Whom shall I send? And who will go for us?"

Even though the "let us" passages were not explicitly mentioned in the New Testament, by the second century, the early church fathers had connected the "let us" passages with the Trinity. For example, commenting on Genesis 1:26, Irenaeus wrote, "Now man is a mixed organization of soul and flesh, who was formed after the likeness of God [the Father], and molded by his hands, that is, by the Son and the Holy Spirit, to whom also he said, 'Let us make man.'"[21]

The New Testament writers explain the Trinity with more clarity and help us understand how the God of Deuteronomy 6:4 ("Hear, O Israel: The LORD our God, the LORD is one")

---

20 Stanley J. Grenz, The Social God and the Relational Self (London: Westminster John Knox Press, 2001), p. 294.

21 Irenaeus, Against Heresies, ed. Alexander Roberts and James Donaldson, Vol. 1, The Ante Nicene Fathers (Grand Rapids, MI: Eerdmans, 1953), preface, sec. 4 as quoted in Peter Toon, Our Triune God (Wheaton, IL: Victor Books), p. 100.

exists in three persons. Torrance reminds us that we only understand the God of the Old Testament through the New Testament's revelation of the Trinity,

> The Trinity is not just a way of thinking about God, for the one true God is actually and intrinsically Triune and cannot be truly conceived otherwise. There is in fact no real knowledge of God as God except through his revealing or naming of himself as Father, Son, and Holy Spirit, for the three Persons are the one true God—apart from them God cannot be known in the truth and reality of his Being.[22]

John 1:1 says that in the beginning was the Word, and the Word was with God, and the Word was God. Then John says in 1:14 that the Word became flesh and lived among us. The New Testament writers give us many other Trinitarian expressions, such as Matthew 3:16-17, "At that moment heaven was opened, and he saw the Spirit of God descending like a dove and lighting on him. And a voice from heaven said, 'This is my Son, whom I love; with him I am well pleased.'" The appearance of all three members is also clearly seen in the famous baptismal formula in Matthew 28:19 when Jesus tells the disciples to baptize future disciples in the name of the Father, Son, and Holy Spirit.

The expression of the Trinity is also seen in 2 Corinthians 13:14, "May the grace of the Lord Jesus Christ, and the love of God, and the fellowship of the Holy Spirit be with you all."

From these Scriptures, and many more like them, it's clear that:

---

22 Torrance, p. 12.

1. The Father is God: "Yet for us there is but one God, the Father, from whom all things came and for whom we live" (1 Corinthians 8:6).
2. Jesus is God: "But about the Son he says, 'Your throne, O God, will last forever and ever'" (Hebrews 1:8).
3. The Holy Spirit is God: Peter says, "Ananias, how is it that Satan has so filled your heart that you have lied to the Holy Spirit . . . You have not lied to men but to God" (Acts 5:3-4).

The overriding view in the Old Testament was that there is only one God. As the early church fathers scrutinized Scripture, three truths emerged:

1. There is only one God
2. God is three persons
3. Each person is fully God

Even though the word *Trinity* is not in the Bible, Scripture teaches the existence of only one God that exists in three persons: Father, Son, and Holy Spirit. The early church concluded in the famous Athanasian Creed (late fifth century AD),

For there is one Person of the Father; another of the Son; and another of the Holy Ghost. But the Godhead of the Father, of the Son, and of the Holy Ghost, is all one: the Glory equal, the Majesty coeternal. Such as the Father is; such is the Son; and such is the Holy Ghost.

The truth is that we can't fully explain the Trinity. God is infinitely greater than we are, and we can't completely understand him. Because of our limitations, illustrations have been used to describe the Trinity. Some are better than others. A widely used illustration is the triangle. One triangle has three corners, which are inseparable from, and identical to, one another. In this sense it is a good illustration of the Trinity. Of course, the triangle is finite and God is infinite.

Augustine, the early church scholar, illustrated the Trinity from 1 John 4:16, which tells us that God is love. Augustine reasoned that love involves a lover, a beloved, and a spirit of love between lover and loved. The Father might be likened to the lover; the Son to the one loved, and the Holy Spirit is the spirit of love. Yet love does not exist unless these three are united as one. This illustration has the advantage of being personal, since it involves love, a characteristic that only flows from persons.

THE GOD OF COMMUNITY

The Trinity dwells in perfect unity and community. God is not a lone individualist, and this fact should stir God's people away from rugged individualism ("How can I do my thing?") to community-oriented living ("How can I serve the body of Christ?"). Tim Keller writes,

> The Augustinian argument says that if God was uni-personal, then there wouldn't have been love until he created somebody. Therefore love would not actually be intrinsic to God. But if you have a God who is tri-personal and therefore in a loving community of relationships from the beginning, then love is at the foundation of everything, and it's the reason we find love to be so important and why relationships are more vital than anything else. To say that

God is loving now, that's one thing. But to say God is love in his very essence, that's another.[23]

As Keller points out, love must be at the foundation of everything we do because the same loving community exists within the Trinity. Relationships must be vital because they are essential to God.

It's doubtful that we can know community and loving relationships apart from the Trinity. In other words, the Trinity is the basis for loving one another. We are relational beings because we are made in the image of a relational God. People are not created to live in isolation or to pursue rugged individualism. In the beginning, God said it was not good for man to be alone. He brought the animals to Adam, but eventually created Eve, so man could also live in community, just as God does.

Jesus often spoke about unity and love, and the New Testament mentions "one another" over fifty times.[24] The reason for this emphasis is because God is Trinity and desires love and unity in the church. The very nature of the Trinity stirs the church to prioritize community. Or, at least it should.

Jesus often pointed to the unity within the Trinity as a model for his disciples to follow. Notice how Jesus describes his relationship to the Father, "That all of them may be one, Father, just as you are in me and I am in you. May they also be in us so that the world may believe that you have sent me. I have given

---

23 Tim Keller, interview, *Servant Magazine* (Three Hills, Alberta Canada), Iss. 88, December 2011, p. 10.

24 See a partial list of the "one another" references in John 13:34, 15:12; Romans 12:10, 12:15, 12:16, 13:8, 14:19; 1 Corinthians 12:25; Galatians 6:2; Ephesians 4:2, 4:25, 4:32, 5:21; Philippians 2:3; Col. 3:13; 1 Thessalonians 3:12, 4:9, 5:11, 5:15; 2 Thessalonians 1:3; 1 Peter 3:8; James 5:16.

them the glory that you gave me, that they may be one as we are one" (John 17:21-22).

The unity of the Father, Son, and Holy Spirit jump out from the pages of Scripture. The New Testament reads like a living love letter between the triune God and his people. The Father loves and delights in the Son (Matthew 3:17). Jesus receives the love of the Father and pleases him out of love and obedience (John 12:26). Jesus says, "When a man believes in me, he does not believe in me only, but in the one who sent me. When he looks at me, he sees the one who sent me" (John 12:44-45).

The Spirit glorifies both the Father and the Son (John 16:14). The Spirit brings back to memory the words of Christ (John 16:12-15). Each person of the Trinity loves, honors, and glorifies the other and receives love and honor in return from the others. Jürgen Moltmann, a theologian who has written on the Trinity in many different volumes, says,

> The three divine persons are not there simply for themselves. They are there in that they are there for one another. They are persons in social relationship. The Father can be called Father only in relationship with the Son; the Son can be called Son only in relationship with the Father. The Spirit is the breath of the one who speaks.[25]

Christ gathered twelve disciples and journeyed with them for three years to demonstrate and teach them about love and community. Their training mainly consisted in learning how to love one another. Jesus had a huge challenge to unite such a diverse group. He brought together disciples who were temperamental and easily offended. They often saw each other

---

25 E. Moltmann-Wendel and J. Moltmann, *Humanity in God* (New York: Pilgrim, 1983), p. 97, as quoted in Julie Gorman, *Community That Is Christian* (Wheaton, IL, Victor Books, 1993), pp. 25-26.

as competitors. It wasn't easy for them to wash each other's feet (John 13:14), but Jesus told them that people outside the community would recognize they were his disciples by the love they had for one another.

The church is a place where the being and nature of God should be demonstrated through loving relationships (Colossians 1:18-19; Ephesians 1:22-23). As the church understands and grows in love with the triune God, it must reflect that same unity in the family of God.

Jürgen Moltmann emphasizes that the absence of the Trinitarian view of God has resulted in the "possessive individualism" in society, which was developed in the midst of the disappearance of the doctrine of the Trinity in the Western world.[26]

Gilbert Bilezikian makes the same case. He writes,

The nature of the Godhead as a plurality of interdependent persons provided the model for relationships among humans. It was not good for the man to be alone because his creation in God's image called for a union of oneness with someone like him. Soon after the creation of human oneness, this interrelational dimension of God's image became the first casualty of the Fall, with the destruction of community.[27]

It's so easy for people to justify their isolation and self-interest by saying, "That's just how I am." However, the Bible, not our

---

26 Jürgen Moltmann, *The Trinity and the Kingdom* (Trinitat und Reich Gottes). Margaret Kohl, trans. New York: Harper and Row Publishers, 1981), pp. 196-200 as quoted in Hae Gyue Kim, *Biblical Foundations for the Cell-Based Churches Applied to the Urban Context of Seoul, Korea* (Pasadena, CA: Fuller Theological Seminary, 2003), p.30.
27 Gilbert Bilezikian, *Community 101* (Grand Rapids, MI: Zondervan, 2009), Kindle locations 896-900.

culture, must direct our thoughts and actions. God's Word governs our lives and guides us into what is right and true. As God is a being, living in a mutually interdependent community, so we humans are created for community. As Richard Meyers says, "We have been given a 'communal gene,' by our Creator."[28] We have been designed and imprinted for relationships.

Individualism might be the cultural norm in the Western world, but God loves community and unity. One of the key values of cell church is that people live in community rather than hide in anonymity. The intimacy of a cell group encourages people to know and be known.

THE TRINITY WORKING IN US

Moving from a life of individualism toward one of community requires a powerful inner transformation. The good news is that God is within believers, molding and shaping them to be more community oriented, to reflect the Trinity's nature. As the Trinity works within believers, they begin to reflect his design for them. This "design" is what Larry Crabb, famous psychologist and popular author, pinpoints,

> We were designed by our Trinitarian God (who is himself a group of three persons in profound relationship with each other) to live in relationship. Without it, we die. It's that simple. Without a community where we know, explore, discover, and touch one another, we experience isolation

---

28 Rev. Richard C. Meyers, *One Anothering, vol. 2* (Philadelphia, PA: Innisfree Press, 1999), p. 20.

and despair that drive us in wrong directions that corrupt our efforts to live meaningfully and to love well. [29]

God not only "designed" believers to be like himself, but he then works within them to fulfill this design. In reality, a personal relationship with God is not really personal. Rather, it's communion with the three-in-one who then transforms believers to be like him. Old Testament scholar, John Goldingay, writes, "Our divinization (our realizing the goal of becoming like God and thus being human) thus consists in our participating in God's existence, having the same kind of personal life as God does."[30] God's personal life within us is communal.

As the Trinity works within us, we can begin fulfilling the "one anothers" of Scripture. Jesus himself says a believer cannot bear fruit by himself; he must remain in the vine to bear fruit. As believers remain in the Trinity, his power and transforming love molds and shapes them to live in love and unity.

I've written extensively about personal devotions and believe strongly in them. The most important book I've written, in fact, is about personal devotions called *An Appointment with the King*. Yet, increasingly I've come to understand that personal devotions are not really personal. Rather, a time of personal devotions is communion with the Trinity, the three-in-one. Devotions are all about growing in a love relationship with a God who does not act independently or in a selfish, individualistic manner. Our relationship with him then overflows to our relationship with others.

As I seek Jesus, I become more like this one who came down to model his own oneness and love with the Father and Spirit.

---

29 As quoted in Randy Frazee, *The Connecting Church* (Grand Rapids, MI: Zondervan, 2001), p. 13.
30 John Goldingay, *Key Questions about Christian Faith* (Grand Rapids, MI: Baker Academic, 2010), p. 50.

During a quiet time, I catch a glimpse of what perfect love and unity is all about. I begin to see others through his eyes. Dietrich Bonhoeffer experienced the horrors of Nazi Germany, the embodiment of human-centered pride. Yet, in the midst of such chaos, Bonhoeffer wrote, *Life Together,* a treatise of God-centered community between believers. He writes,

> The believer therefore lauds the Creator, the Redeemer, God, Father, Son, and Holy Spirit, for the bodily presence of a brother. The prisoner, the sick person, the Christian in exile sees in the companionship of a fellow Christian a physical sign of the gracious presence of the triune God.[31]

God helps us see his presence in others and to love them like he does. We begin to see how he is molding people and transforming them into his image. Community, in fact, is the very nature of God.

---

31 Dietrich Bonhoeffer, *Life Together* (New York: Harper & Row, 1954), p. 20.

Chapter Three

THE FAMILY OF GOD

In the creation story of Genesis 1, God looked over all of his creation and declared it to be "'very good" (verse 31). Each part of the creation was perfect because God made it. However, there was one missing ingredient: community.

God's creation of the first human, like the rest of his creation, was perfectly designed. Made in God's image, the human creation could think, feel, and act, just like God. But he couldn't do one thing: he could not interact and enjoy communion, like his triune Creator, because there was no one to communicate with. God said in Genesis 2:18 "It is not good for the man to be alone." Although God made various creatures to interact with Adam, they didn't provide the community he needed. In other words, the animal creation was not able to provide the community and interaction that Adam required. So God created Eve, who enjoyed communion with Adam and completed him.

Adam and Eve gave birth to children and the family was born. Through the family, God wanted to display the community that exists within his triune nature. Although sin tainted family values and corrupted the course of history, God persisted to show his love to the families he created.

When family is in a right relationship with God, it's a beautiful thing. When sin and selfishness reign, family relationships disintegrate. With the entrance of sin in Genesis 3, we see family lines characterized by pride, turmoil, and destruction. Yet, the story of the Old Testament centers on God's love for the family, and how he strove to reach out to his creation.

FAMILY HOUSEHOLDS

The first families after Adam and Eve saw themselves as rivals, rather than co-workers. The selfishness and disunity caused the first families to stray so far away from their Creator that God decided to start over. God brought Noah and his house into the ark, along with his sons and their wives (Genesis 5-6). God saved these families to start over based on a new covenant of love and commitment.

When Noah and his family left the ark, Noah made a covenant with God, and God made a commitment with Noah. He says to Noah and his family, "Be fruitful and multiply, and fill the earth, and subdue it; and have dominion" (Genesis 1:28; 9:1). God continued his plan of family reproduction in spite of continued strife and power struggles (e.g., tower of Babel in Genesis 11). In keeping with his promise, rather than destroying his erring creation, God chose a new family lineage in Abram (Genesis 12:1-3).

He commanded Abram to leave his ancestral home, so he could break away from the old, corrupted community in which he lived to lay the foundations for a new one. God gave Abram the promise of a personal blessing ("I will bless you"), which would translate into a national blessing ("I will make you into a great nation"). By leaving his old, broken-down community and by going toward a land of promise, Abram accepted God's plan to establish a new community that would eventually bring together, in the church, believers from all the peoples of the earth.[32]

Through the lineage of Abraham's son, Isaac, God continued to bless and multiply families. Jacob, Isaac's son and heir of God's promise, established his family which extended into an entire household. As Jacob and his family traveled from Paddan Aram to the promised land, God encountered Jacob and changed his name to Israel. Israel's household lived together in families—all twelve households along with their families. In fact, it was common for families in Old Testament times to live together in larger households.

When we think of families today, we think of our modern concept of nuclear families. However, in Old Testament times, households were much more extensive. Leo G. Perdue, a scholar on ancient Israel, writes,

Family households did not consist of nuclear families in the modern understanding of a married couple and their children but rather were multigenerational (up to four generations) and included the social arrangement of several families, related by blood and marriage, who lived in two or three houses architecturally connected. [33]

---

32 Bilezikian, pp. 31-32.
33 Leo G. Perdue, Joseph Blenkinsopp, John J. Collins, and Carol Meyers, *Families in Ancient Israel* (Louisville, KY: Westminster John Knox Press, 1997), pp. 174-175.

The generations living in these households would spread over several dwelling places.[34] In our modern society, we are accustomed to urban life, but the Old Testament context was mainly rural. The people lived in villages. Carol Meyers writes, "Most settlements of the early Israelite period were small, rural sites. Certainly for that period . . . the primary locus of family life was the village."[35] It's been estimated that a normal size village might have been fifty people, whereas a large one would have about one hundred fifty people.[36]

Those who formed part of the kinship grouping back then were focused on the entire family, rather than their individual needs. As a group-oriented, collective culture, economic survival extended beyond the individual household to the clans, tribes, and all the children of Israel. Perdue writes,

The modern concept of individualism was not known in ancient Israel and early Judaism, though a basic understanding of individual responsibility within the larger corporate whole began to develop during the exilic period (Ezekiel 19). On the whole, however, the strong sense of corporate solidarity and community dominated Israel's and early Judaism's social and religious world. The social and economic interdependence of members of the household produced the understanding of corporate identity and community that shaped people's relationships and lives. In the household, individual will and needs merged into the collective will and needs of the larger whole. The behavior of the individual affected the whole, and this was especially true of the head of the household, who embodied within

---

34 Goldingay, p. 289.
35 Perdue, Blenkinsopp, Collins, and Meyers, p. 12.
36 Ibid., p. 12.

himself the whole of the household (Ex. 20:5-6; Josh. 7:16-26). This collective good transcended the good of any individual member.[37]

The marriages were arranged by the parents of the two households, and the sons and daughters were not always consulted (Genesis 21:21; 34: 4-6; 38:6; Joshua 15:16; 1 Samuel 18:17-27; 25:44). Incest and marrying outside the tribal boundaries were strictly forbidden (Leviticus 18, 20; Exodus 34:11-16; Numbers 25:1-2; Deuteronomy 7:3-4; Judges 3:5-6; Nehemiah 13:23-27).

Group hospitality was highly valued and practiced among Old Testament households. Strangers could expect attention and care for long periods of time. Christine D. Pohl writes,

The Old Testament legacy of hospitality is instructive for us. First, the household into which a stranger was welcomed was the center of both social and family activity. Second, even in the earliest part of the tradition, care for strangers went beyond the household. It involved community responsibility and provision, and depended on legislation as well as on generous individual responses. There was never an assumption that individual households alone could care for large numbers of needy strangers. Third, strangers were often first encountered in a more public space. Such a setting allowed a preliminary interaction that reduced some of their "strangeness" before they entered a household. It also provided the larger community with an opportunity to encounter the stranger.[38]

---

37 Perdue, Blenkinsopp, Collins, and Meyers, p. 237.
38 Christine D. Pohl. *Making Room: Recovering Hospitality as a Christian Tradition* (Grand Rapids, MI: Eerdmans, 1999), p. 41.

The household provided the care network for not only those related by marriage but also those who were marginalized and needed special assistance.

God's triune community nature was reflected in group outreach to strangers, the homeless, and those in need. While loving all people, God continued to focus on his chosen family, the Israelites.

Family Expansion

God's family grew and prospered in Egypt under Joseph's oversight. Their incredible growth, however, threatened the new Pharaoh, and God led his family out of Egypt in fulfilling his role as Israel's Father. God says to them later, "You yourselves have seen what I did to Egypt, and how I carried you on eagles' wings and brought you to myself" (Exodus 19:4).

According to Exodus 12:37-38, the Israelites numbered "about six hundred thousand men on foot, besides women and children," plus many non-Israelites and livestock. Numbers 1:46 gives a more precise total of six hundred three thousand five hundred fifty. The six hundred thousand, plus wives, children, the elderly, and the "mixed multitude" of non-Israelites would have numbered approximately two million people (a more conservative estimate of 1.5 million is often used), which compares to the size of Houston or Philadelphia, respectively.

As this huge family journeyed from Egypt, it soon became apparent that they needed to re-organize. Jethro, Moses' father-in-law, seeing Moses' desperate situation, counseled him to raise up leaders to care for the thousands, hundreds, and tens of people. Jethro summed up the problem succinctly, "You are wearying yourself and also those who hear you" (Exodus 18:18). Moses tried to be a responsible leader, but it was too much for him to do alone. Jethro recounted the advantages of this leadership approach to Moses, "You will be able to stand the strain, and all these people will go home satisfied" (Exodus 18:23).

Assuming a more conservative estimate of 1.5 million Israelites, this would mean there were one hundred fifty thousand family units (groups of ten), thirty thousand clusters of fifties, six thousand clusters of hundreds, and according to Exodus 24:9, seventy leaders who would have been over the thousands.

We often use the word "nation" to describe Israel, but we must remember that they were organized according to families, clans, and tribes. It was through this intimate web of household and tribal organization that any person could be singled out for inspection. There are various examples of winnowing out one person by tribe, clan, and families. When Achan disobeyed, we read:

Early the next morning Joshua had Israel come forward by tribes, and Judah was taken. The clans of Judah came forward, and he took the Zerahites. He had the clan of the Zerahites come forward by families, and Zimri was taken. Joshua had his family come forward man by man, and Achan son of Carmi, the son of Zimri, the son of Zerah, of the tribe of Judah, was taken (Joshua 7:16-18).

Even with such a large number of people, God organized them according to family units. God then cared for each unit through an organizational supervisory structure that many in today's cell church call the *Jethro Model*. The family was the base of this care structure because this was God's design from the beginning.

Family Failure

The Israelites were supposed to demonstrate God's divine nature and unity to the nations. Sadly, the Israelites failed in this task, bickering among themselves and straying from the one who called them.

Yet, even in those dire conditions, the prophets envisioned Israel as a family, a household that would be restored. In Hosea 1-3, relations within the family provide the metaphor for their coming destiny. The prophets spoke out against wayward families, knowing that when a man is wayward, the children share in the trouble (Amos 7:17). Yet God says that even if the Israelite family were destroyed, it would also be rebuilt (Ezekiel 37:11-14). And a remnant of Israel did emerge to rebuild and restore the family connection (Nehemiah and Ezra).

JESUS AND THE NEW FAMILY OF GOD

Jesus came to start a new community, the new family of God (Matthew 12:46-50). Although the definition of the church needed further explanation, Jesus formed his new family by asking them to break with the old and make a total commitment to follow him. Joseph Hellerman in *When the Church Was a Family*, writes,

He [Jesus] chose "family" as the defining metaphor to describe His followers . . . one's family demanded the highest commitment of undivided loyalty, relational solidarity, and personal sacrifice of any social entity in Jesus' strong-group Mediterranean world. And the major life decisions were made in the context of the family.[39]

---

39 Joseph Hellerman, *When the Church Was a Family* (Nashville, TN: B&H Academic, 2009), p. 31.

Jesus himself says in Mark 10:29-31,

> No one who has left home or brothers or sisters or mother or father or children or fields for me and the gospel will fail to receive a hundred times as much in this present age (homes, brothers, sisters, mothers, children and fields—and with them, persecutions) and in the age to come, eternal life. But many who are first will be last, and the last first.

Following Jesus meant leaving all behind and starting afresh. Gerhard Lohfink writes, "Those who follow Jesus . . . allow themselves to be gathered by Jesus into a 'new family' that stands entirely under the sign of the reign of God."[40]

Following Jesus was especially difficult in the collective culture of the New Testament because people saw themselves as part of the group. A person's identity was collective, so following Jesus meant breaking with family, friends, and religion to follow Christ and his followers.[41] Ritva Williams writes,

> The Jesus movement was born in a group-oriented world where the household/family was regarded as the very basis of social life. . . . The group that gathered around Jesus in his lifetime consisted of family members, most frequently siblings and/or their mothers, who left the households of their fathers and husbands. In the Jesus movement they found a surrogate family.[42]

---

40 Gerhard Lohfink, *Does God Need the Church?* (Collegeville, MN: The Liturgical Press, 1998), p. 132.

41 Hellerman, p. 6.

42 Ritva H. Williams, *Stewards, Prophets, Keepers of the Word* (Peabody, MA: Hendrickson Publishers, 2006), p. 30.

Jesus often taught in homes to communicate to his followers what his new family would look like. He came to create a new, transformed people who were brothers and sisters. Although Jesus used the household family network that existed at the time, he transformed it with a new vision for love and sacrifice. He cemented the new concept of family by living among them and showing them how to love and serve one another (John 13:1-17).

Christ's teaching on true greatness (using children as an example) takes place in the context of a house setting (Mark 9:33-36). The new family that Christ envisioned would have servanthood as its central leadership style and childlike dependence as the guiding light.[43] Then he sent his disciples two by two to engage and infiltrate the heart of the culture: the family. The disciples went into the houses and transformed unbelievers from the inside out.

Jesus wanted his new family to enjoy the oneness he experienced with the father—a oneness that had originally been entrusted in creation, and already existed within the Trinity. For Jesus, the model for oneness among humans was the relationship between Father and Son (John 17:11, 21, 22). Referring to their oneness, the Son declared to the Father, "You are in me and I am in you," and he could pray for his followers to be one to the same extent and with the same intensity (17:21). In his final prayer, Christ extends his concern for oneness to all believers of all times throughout the future of the church (17:20).[44]

---

43 Carolyn Osiek, Margaret Y. MacDonald, Janet H. Tulloch, *A Women's Place: House Churches in Earliest Christianity* (Minneapolis, MI: Augsburg Fortress, 2006), Kindle edition, p. 83.
44 Bilezikian, p. 36.

THE CHURCH AS GOD'S FAMILY

The Jesus strategy of house to house ministry and the early house church environment combined to create the atmosphere from which the theological doctrine of the family of God emerged. The early disciples were simply following their master in emphasizing the new family of God based in homes. [45]

The metaphors "God the Father," "Jesus the Son," "children of God," "brothers and sisters in Christ," along with a number of other family terms became a means to communicate a new Christian theology. It also built a foundation of church community and interactions between its members. Paul uses the terms "brothers," "sisters," some one hundred eighteen times in his letters. [46] Robert Banks writes,

> The comparison of the Christian community with a "family" must be regarded as the most significant metaphorical usage of all. For that reason it has pride of place in this discussion. More than any of the other images utilized by Paul, it reveals the essence of this thinking about community.[47]

In Ephesians 3:14-15 Paul says, "For this reason I kneel before the Father, from whom his whole family in heaven and on earth derives its name." He was writing to the house churches in Ephesus and wanted believers to know their inheritance as the family of God, called and specifically chosen by God. Goetzmann writes, "What could be conveyed by the idea of

---

45 Robert Banks, *Paul's Idea of Community* (Peabody, MA: Hendrickson Publications, 1994), p. 56.
46 Williams, p. 34.
47 Banks, p. 49.

the family of God had, in fact, already come into being in the primitive Christian community through the house churches."[48]

The household setting confirmed that believers were God's family. In the heavily group-oriented Mediterranean world of the first century, the family was the most significant group. Belonging to a family provided the main focus for identity and at the same time, if that family were regarded as honorable, the person's identity was enhanced.[49] Hellerman says,

> The most important group for persons in the ancient world was the family. It is hardly accidental that the New Testament writers chose the concept of family as the central social metaphor to describe the kind of interpersonal relationships that were to characterize those early Christian communities. There is, in fact, no better way to come to grips with the spiritual and relational poverty of American individualism than to compare our way of doing things with the strong-group, surrogate family relations of early Christianity.[50]

The family image probably made a lot of sense to those early believers, because as Halvor Moxnes points out, "In the traditional Mediterranean culture, the family was the basic reference of the individual, and the channel through which he or she was inserted into social life. To be born in a certain family was a decisive factor, because family was the depository of 'honor' and of position in society, and the transmitter of

---

48 J. Goetzmann, "House," *The New International Dictionary of the New Testament,* vol. 2. Colin Brown, ed. (Grand Rapids, MI: Zondervan, 1975), p. 250.
49 Philip F. Esler, "Family Imagery and Christian Identify in Gal 5:13 to 6:10" in *Constructing Early Christian Families,* Halvor Moxnes, ed. (London: Routledge, 1997), p. 131.
50 Hellerman, p. 6.

economic resources."[51] It was in this family setting that a person found his or her sense of belonging. As Williams writes, "Without a family, without kin, one is nobody."[52]

GOD'S HOUSEHOLD

"The family of God" and "household of God" are both used in the New Testament to describe Christ's church. These two terms are the principal church images of the New Testament. They reflect two sides of the same coin and both extend from the house church. Helen Doohan writes,

Closely associated with the household image is the description of the church as family. Paul describes his relationship with the churches in terms drawn from family life, such as father (1 Cor. 4:14-15), mother (Gal. 4:19), nurse (1 Cor. 3:2), speaking in tender and endearing ways. The family reveals the essence of Paul's thinking about community. Use of the homes of Christians for the gathering of the community reflects the family character of the early church. The atmosphere and attitudes in the community speak to fundamental family values, with trust, respect, love, patience, tolerance, resilience, and generosity, ensuring the kind of interaction essential to being church.[53]

---

51 Halvor Moxnes, ed., *Constructing Early Christian Families* (London: Routledge, 1997), p. 62. .

52 Williams, p. 38

53 Helen Doohan, *Paul's Vision of Church* (Wilmington, DE: Good News Publisher, 1989), p. 143.

Although household and family are connected terms, the "household of God" goes beyond the idea of nuclear family and helps focus on the extended family.[54] The authors of *Home Cell Groups and House Churches* explain,

Paul's letters contain a number of figures of speech to describe the nature and function of the church. A major metaphor is that of a household, a family. This figure conveys an idea which has a deep rootage in the Old Testament where God's people are often referred to in a variety of family-oriented figures. In writing to Timothy, Paul referred to the church as the "household of God" (1 Timothy 3:15). He used the same language in writing to the Ephesian Christians (Ephesians 2:19). In Galatians 6:10, Paul changed the language slightly and referred to the church as the "household of faith."[55]

The household in the New Testament was the center of Christian ministry. It provided worship, recruitment, mutual support, and the basis for the social embodiment of the gospel message. Paul says in 1 Timothy 3:15, "If I am delayed, you will know how people ought to conduct themselves in God's household, which is the church of the living God, the pillar and foundation of the truth." In this verse, Paul extends the image of the house church to the church at large. Gehring says,

Scholars have correctly declared 1 Timothy 3:15 to be the central ecclesiological passage . . . The understanding of the church here goes beyond the metaphorical; the church

54 Moxnes, p. 29.
55 C. Kirk Hadaway, Francis M. DuBose, Stuart A. Wright, *Home Cell Groups and House Churches* (Nashville, TN: Broadman Press, 1987), p. 57.

is characterized, in its concrete organizational structures, by the perception of itself as a household, with the "household" understood in terms of the ancient *oikos*. For the Pastorals the church really is the household or the family of God. Viewed in this way, "house or family of God" becomes the model for responsible behavior as well as for church order and leadership structures, and thus the central, all-guiding image for the self-understanding and organization of the church.[56]

The designation of the church as the "house of God" was understood by all the house church members quite literally. The image of the house is molded together with the family of God. To understand the church as God's house also meant that God himself was the head of the church.

In 2 Timothy 2:20-21, the members of the church are described as objects in a large house. The local church leader (overseer) is the house administrator (Titus 1:7). This overseer is supposed to carry out the functions of the householder (1 Timothy 3:5) in the church of God, in that he manages, leads, corrects, and so forth. Dunn summarizes succinctly, "The model of the well-run household provided precedent for the well-run church."[57] Gehring says,

It was quite natural that household patterns impressed themselves upon the social reality of the congregation. The house churches of the Pastoral Letters understood themselves essentially as the "household or family of

---

56 Gehring, p. 261.
57 J. Dunn, *Colossians, Philemon*, 245, as quoted in Roger W. Gehring, *House Church and Mission: The Importance of Household Structures in Early Christianity* (Peabody, MA: Hendrickson, 2004), p. 260.

God," and it is therefore fully legitimate to speak here of an *oikos* ecclesiology.[58]

The family/household image naturally found its way into the mentality of the New Testament house churches. Only those who manage their own households in an exemplary fashion can be trusted to manage the church (1 Timothy 3:5), and they must set an example in having "submissive and respectful children" (1 Timothy 3:4), that is, specifically, children who are "believers" (Titus 1:6).[59]

Because leadership developed naturally within the house church setting, people could examine whether or not the members were guiding their own families in a godly, Christlike manner. Those who were godly examples to both family and outsiders were the ones called upon to lead God's household, the church of the living God.

FAMILY INSTRUCTION

In New Testament times, the basic family group living in the same house consisted of father, mother, the unmarried children, probably one or more married sons with their own wives and children, and often workers and slaves.

Because the early church was organized around this extended family, the need arose for specific teaching on how to behave as the new, transformed family of God. In his letters to the house churches in Colossae and Ephesus, Paul includes

---

58 Gehring, p. 298.
59 John M.G. Barclay, "The Family as the Bearer of Religion in Judaism and Early Christianity," in *Constructing Early Christian Families*, Halvor Moxnes, ed. (London: Routledge, 1997), p. 77.

instructions (often called the household codes) on how the family-oriented house churches should behave (Colossians 3:18 ff and Ephesians 5:22 ff).

Fathers, mothers, and children are all exhorted to care for one another and fulfill their roles within the family. John Barclay writes, "The household code assumes the solidarity of a Christian family, and projects an image of the household as the context in which Christian discipleship is given practical expression."[60] Paul gave his instructions to:

- Husbands and wives (Ephesians 5:22-33; Colossians 3:18-19)
- Parents and children (Ephesians 6:1-4; Colossians 3:20- 21)
- Masters and slaves (Ephesians 6:5-9; Colossians 3:22-4:1)

We know that children were present in those early house church meetings both through church history and also because Paul mentions children in his letters. Osiek, MacDonald, and Tulloch write,

That children were not merely chance witnesses at early Christian meetings but actually expected to be active listeners to early Christian discourse is made clear by the direct address to them (along with other family groupings) in the New Testament household codes (Col. 3:20; Eph. 6:1).[61]

---

60 Barclay, p. 76.
61 Osiek, MacDonald, Tulloch, Kindle edition, pp. 70-71.

Many of the children addressed in the household codes of Colossians and Ephesians were probably slave children (some with no knowledge of or contact with biological parents), and many of the adult slaves who were instructed no doubt had children.[62]

In the Roman world, the role of motherhood was often shared by a variety of people, including nurses, caregivers, and surrogate parents of various kinds. Osiek, MacDonald, and Tulloch write,

> There must have been many cases in which children (especially of lower status) ended up, for all practical purposes, in the care of others, adopted by default; these orphan children may have been habitually fed, occasionally washed, and put to bed by different people. If we add to this the strong possibility that rescuing abandoned children would have been understood as an act of Christian charity . . . we end up with the likelihood that widows often were caring for children who were not their own. The second-century depictions of early Christian groups welcoming ragamuffin children with slaves and women in tow, therefore, was probably not too far off the mark—especially if one observed the 'orphans and widow' from an outsider's perspective. [63]

Paul gave his instructions in the plural to clarify that the rules are directed not only toward the one master, wife, children, and servants in one household, but rather toward all members in all households and all house churches—everyone in the entire church as a whole at that location.

---

62 Ibid., pp. 73-74.
63 Ibid., pp. 76-77.

The strengthening of the family simultaneously strengthened the house churches. A well-functioning household can only exist upon the foundation of a healthy, intact family, and so a close connection existed between the family and the New Testament house church.

FAMILY HOSPITALITY

Hospitality portrayed the message of God's love through the new family of God. Because the early church met in homes, hospitality was a natural and necessary practice. It helped to foster family-like ties among believers and provided a setting in which to shape and to reinforce a new identity.[64]

Paul encourages the church in Rome to practice hospitality (Romans 12:13), the writer of Hebrews reminds believers not to neglect hospitality (Hebrews 13:1-3), and Peter challenges the community to offer hospitality ungrudgingly (1 Peter 4:9). Hospitality, in each of these passages, is a concrete expression of love for the household of God and beyond to strangers, just as we see in the Old Testament. Osiek, MacDonald, and Tulloch write, "Hospitality emerges early as a key virtue in early Christian groups, as is demonstrated by the very hospitality offered by the missionary couple to Paul himself (Acts 18:1-3; see Romans 12:13; Hebrews 13:1-3)."[65]

The gospel initially spread through believers who traveled widely and depended on the hospitality of others. The travel of church members and their ministry involvement would not have been possible without the assistance from believers. Paul

---

64 Pohl, pp. 31-32.
65 Osiek, MacDonald, Tulloch, pp. 31-32.

asked Philemon to prepare quarters for him in his own house because he, like other traveling missionaries, depended on the homes of the early Christian believers (Philemon 22).

Such hospitality was not only practical, but was seen as actually participating in the gospel ministry. John the apostle says, "You are faithful in what you are doing for the brothers, even though they are strangers to you. . . . It was for the sake of the Name that they went out, receiving no help from the pagans. We ought therefore to show hospitality to such men so that we may work together for the truth" (3 John 1:5-8).

On the other hand, John also warned believers not to participate in the false ministries of anti-Christs and deceivers, writing, "Do not take him into your house or welcome him. Anyone who welcomes him shares in his wicked work" (2 John 1:10-11).

Hospitality to those first missionaries and the reception of their message were very closely connected. Jesus set the standard for the church in this regard, by sending his twelve and his seventy-two disciples out from village to village and house-to-house to bring the kingdom of God into their midst, reminding his disciples that those who accepted them, in fact, were accepting him and the good news of the gospel (Luke 9:1-6; 10:1-11). In Romans 15:7, Paul urges believers to "welcome one another" as Christ welcomed them. Jesus' gracious and sacrificial hospitality, which was expressed in his life, ministry, and death, serves as the basis for hospitality among his followers.

Most of the ancient world regarded hospitality as a fundamental moral practice. It was necessary for the protection of vulnerable strangers and assured strangers at least a minimum of provision, protection, and connection with the larger community. It also sustained the normal network of relationships on which a community depended.[66]

This generous hospitality and love among the believers was attractive to unbelievers. Reta Finger writes,

> What attracted people to the community? In a crowded city where most people lived marginal and often desperate lives, many cut off from previous kin-groups back on the land, Luke has truthfully portrayed what was probably one of the great attractions of the new movement: the inclusive and joyful daily communal meals held in the next courtyard.[67]

One principal way to offer hospitality was through eating meals together. Eating together in the household was one of the primary ways to share life together as well as to welcome strangers and those outside the household. Luke declared in Acts 4:34, "There was not a needy person among them."[68]

We like to quote Acts 2:46 concerning the Lord's Supper in the homes of believers, but we are less likely to talk about Acts 2:45, "Selling their possessions and goods, they gave to anyone as he had need." Not only was the breaking of bread in the homes of believers a way to celebrate the Lord's death, it was also a means to make sure no one went away hungry.

Unlike the church in Jerusalem, the church in Corinth was not celebrating the Lord's Supper in the same way. They were not concerned about feeding the poor. Paul writes, "When you come together, it is not the Lord's Supper you eat, for as you eat, each of you goes ahead without waiting for anybody else.

---

66 Pohl, p. 17.
67 Reta Halteman Finger, *Of Widows and Meals: Communal Meals in the Book of Acts* (Grand Rapids, MI: William B. Eerdmans, 2007), p. 244.
68 Ibid., p. 6.

One remains hungry, another gets drunk" (1 Corinthians 11:20-21).

In the early church, believers gave and served to be like Jesus. After all, Jesus washed the feet of his disciples, told them to do likewise, and then said to them, "A new command I give you: Love one another. As I have loved you, so you must love one another. By this all men will know that you are my disciples, if you love one another" (John 13:34-35).

GOD'S FAMILY PLAN

God's plan throughout the ages is to call out a people to model his triune nature of love, unity, and purity. Even though Israel failed to exemplify this community, God's plan did not fail. His family plan continued with Christ and the church. In fact, the primary image of Christ's church is the family of God. But how does Christ's radical call to discipleship and kingdom message relate to this new family?

Chapter Four

REVELATION:
JESUS AND HIS METHOD
OF MINISTRY

Jesus made an impression wherever he went. Some declared him Lord while others mocked him as demon possessed or deranged. Jesus wanted people to decide. He says to his disciples,

> "Who do people say the Son of Man is?" They replied, "Some say John the Baptist; others say Elijah; and still others, Jeremiah or one of the prophets." "But what about you?" he asked. "Who do you say I am?" Simon Peter answered, "You are the Christ, the Son of the living God." Jesus replied, "Blessed are you, Simon son of Jonah, for this was not revealed to you by man, but by my Father in heaven" (Matthew 16:13-17).

Jesus did not leave room for people to remain neutral. He challenged people to be for him or against him, and for this reason some of his own disciples turned away, not being able to accept his sayings (John 6:66). In his book, *Mere Christianity*, C.S. Lewis notes that Jesus never allows himself to be viewed as just a good person. He's either a liar, lunatic, or the Lord of all creation.

According to the gospel of John, Jesus is the God-man who both made the world and then came to save it. John says,

He was in the world, and though the world was made through him, the world did not recognize him. He came to that which was his own, but his own did not receive him. Yet to all who received him, to those who believed in his name, he gave the right to become children of God (John 1:10-12).

Through his teaching and lifestyle Jesus announced that things would never be the same, the old was out and the new had arrived. As N.T. Wright succinctly writes, "He intended it to be clear, that this wasn't just a foretaste of a future reality. This was reality itself. This was what it looked like when God was in charge."[69] Christ's presence on the earth was announcing a new kind of family, a new way of life.

A NEW KINGDOM

Christ's first proclamation was about the kingdom. The Scripture tells us that after John was put in prison, Jesus went into Galilee,

---

69 N.T. Wright, *Simply Jesus: A New Vision of Who He Was, What He Did, and Why He Matters* (New York: Harper Collins, 2011), Kindle locations 2007-2023.

proclaiming the good news of God. "The time has come," he says. "The kingdom of God is near. Repent and believe the good news!" (Mark 1:14-15). What did Jesus mean by the kingdom of God?

We know that the Jews longed for a new social order—one that was free from Roman tyranny and slavery. Christ's disciples expected Jesus, the Messiah, to overthrow the Roman rule and set up a new kingdom. So why didn't he do it? Why didn't he simply fulfill the expectations of the people?

George Eldon Ladd, an early authority on kingdom teaching, explains that the kingdom came in the person of Jesus Christ, but would be fully experienced in the future.[70] For example, in Luke 17:20-21, Jesus declares, ". . . the kingdom of God is within you." An alternative reading to "within you" is "among you." Ladd concludes that Jesus meant "among you." In other words, in the person of Jesus Christ, God's kingdom is now present. Ladd writes, "The age to come has overlapped with this age."[71]

In Matthew 12:28 , Jesus says to the unbelieving Pharisees, "But if I drive out demons by the Spirit of God, then the kingdom of God has come upon you." Christ's authority over sin, sickness, and the demonic were a sign that the kingdom was here. N.T. Wright writes, "He never performed mighty works simply to impress. He saw them as part of the inauguration of the sovereign and healing rule of Israel's covenant God."[72] God had broken into the human realm through the person of Jesus Christ. The kingdom had come. Johannes Verkuyl writes,

---

70 George Eldon Ladd, *The Gospel of the Kingdom* (Grand Rapids, MI: Eerdmans, 1959), p. 42.

71 Ibid., p. 127.

72 N.T. Wright, *Jesus and the Victory of God* (Minneapolis, MN: Fortress Press, 1996), p. 191.

Jesus' miracles . . . provide special help in understanding how the kingdom is revealed in this world. John's Gospel calls the miracles signs which point to the approaching kingdom and majestic character of the Messiah. These miracles address every human need: poverty, sickness, hunger, sin, demonic temptation, and the threat of death. By them Jesus is anticipating Easter. Each of them proclaims that wherever and whenever in God's name human needs and problems are tackled and overcome, there God's kingdom is shining through.[73]

Jesus was not passive toward human needs and suffering. He fed the hungry (Matthew 15:29-39), healed the sick (Matthew 9:35), spoke against oppression (Matthew 21:12-17; 23:1-38), and ended up dying on the cross for the sins of the world (1 John 2:2). Jesus himself declared, "If the world hates you, keep in mind that it hated me first. . . . If I had not come and spoken to them, they would not be guilty of sin. Now, however, they have no excuse for their sin" (John 15:18-25).

JESUS MODELED THE KINGDOM COMMUNITY FOR HIS TWELVE

Why did Jesus choose twelve? New Testament scholars agree that the actual number twelve reflects the fact that Israel was comprised of twelve tribes, and Jesus was inaugurating the reign of God's kingdom. Gerhard Lohfink writes, "The twelve are chosen out of a much larger number of disciples. They represent

73 Johannes Verkuyl, *Contemporary Missiology: An Introduction* (Grand Rapids, MI: Eerdmans, 1981), as quoted in *Perspectives on the World Christian Movement, Eds.* Ralph D. Winter & Steven C. Hawthorne (Pasadena, CA: William Carey Library, 1978), p. 42.

the twelve tribes; they are the beginning and center of growth for the renewed eschatological Israel."[74]

Yet, on another level, Jesus concentrated on the twelve to model community. These twelve men discovered that community can be a difficult place to mask limitations, egotism, ignorance, and jealousies. Try as hard as they could, they were unable to conceal their selfishness. Slowly they recognized they had to abandon their competitive lifestyles.

The greatest among them would be the one who became the servant of all. They discovered that their true worth was not their reputation, but their readiness to give themselves unsparingly to others. By living with twelve men, God in human flesh made a clear statement about the way community develops.

We can also learn much from the way he taught them. He did not simply gather them once a week for a "discipleship class." He lived with them. They stayed in homes, visited Jerusalem, and camped in the mountains. They shared their financial resources.

Jesus didn't only teach his disciples about prayer. He also asked them to accompany him to prayer meetings. He allowed his disciples to see him praying. When the disciples finally asked him what he was doing, he seized upon the opportunity to teach them about prayer (Luke 11:1-4).

Instead of offering a class on hermeneutics or exegesis, Jesus quoted Scripture in his dialogue and then explained the Scripture's meaning (there are sixty-six references to the Old Testament in his dialogue with the disciples).

The same is true with evangelism. Jesus evangelized in the presence of his disciples and then instructed them afterwards. He took advantage of real life situations to carefully explain complex doctrinal issues (e.g., the rich young ruler in Matthew 19:23).

---

74 Lohfink, p. 131.

Christ knew that theoretical information separated from practical experience would have little lasting value. After Christ's disciples finished their ministry tour, they met with Jesus to discuss what happened. The apostles gathered around Jesus and reported to him all they had done and taught (Mark 6:30).

On another occasion, the disciples reported to Jesus, "Lord, even the demons submit to us in your name" (Luke 10:17). Jesus seized the opportunity to instruct them further and to offer additional guidelines, "Do not rejoice that the spirits submit to you, but rejoice that your names are written in heaven" (Luke 10:20).

Christ was constantly reviewing the experiences of his disciples and then offering additional commentary (Mark 9:17-29; 6:30-44). Jesus

- gave the disciples experiences and allowed them to make personal observations
- used the experiences and observations as a starting point to teach a lesson
- modeled what it means to love God and love people by personal example

The disciples learned while doing, but they were also guided to carefully reflect on what they did. Jesus modeled this to his disciples.

CHRIST INITIATED A HOME-BASED MOVEMENT

I sometimes picture Jesus sleeping around campfires, like images of cowboys in the wild, wild West. Yet Jesus ministered in a household setting. When reading about Jesus going from village to village and healing the sick, he was actually ministering in homes. The following offers a glimpse of Christ's home ministry:

- Jesus in the house of Peter (Matthew 8:14)
- Jesus in the house of Matthew (Matthew 9:10)
- Jesus in the house of Zacchaeus (Luke 19:1-10)
- Jesus in the house of Lazarus and his sisters (Luke 10:38-42)
- Jesus in the house of Jairus (Mark 5:35-38)
- Jesus healing two blind people in a house (Matthew 9:28-30)
- Jesus in the house of Simon the leper (Matthew 26:6)
- Jesus teaching his disciples in a house (Mark 7:17-18; 9:33, 10:10)
- Jesus forgiving and healing a paralyzed person in a house (Luke 5:19)
- Jesus in the home of a Pharisee (Luke 14:1)
- Jesus instituting the Lord's Supper in a house (Matthew 26:18)
- Jesus sent his twelve and his seventy disciples to heal and teach from village to village and house-to-house (Luke 9:1-9; 10:1-11)

Christ's original movement was established in the rural culture of that day. Ritva Williams writes, "We need to picture the Jesus movement in rural Galilee and the surrounding region as operating frequently, if not primarily, within and around houses."[75] Ten of the twelve disciples were from Galilee. Only later in the final days of his Jerusalem ministry did he minister in a city environment.

While in Galilee, the house of Peter appears to have been the base of operation. Luke 4:38-40 says,

---

75 Williams, p. 11.

Jesus left the synagogue and went to the home of Simon. Now Simon's mother-in-law was suffering from a high fever, and they asked Jesus to help her. So he bent over her and rebuked the fever, and it left her. She got up at once and began to wait on them. When the sun was setting, the people brought to Jesus all who had various kinds of sickness, and laying his hands on each one, he healed them.

Not only did Peter and Andrew live there, but probably a network of evangelistic contacts grew from that home (e.g., Peter's mother-in-law and wife), including friends of the family. Most likely Peter's house was a place where Jesus and his disciples could pray, enjoy community, and develop spiritually. It also served as a meeting room and place of healing and instruction. In one sense, it was a prototypical house church.[76]

In addition to the house of Peter in Capernaum, we know of Jesus' followers in Bethany. In Jericho, we read of Zacchaeus, the head of a household who became a follower of Jesus (Luke 19:1-10). It's likely that Jesus originally won some of these disciples through house-to-house ministry (Luke 10:5-6).

Many of these followers lived in Galilee (Mark 1:29-31), Judea (Matthew 24:16), and in the Decapolis region (Mark 5:19-20). Gehring writes, "If our perspective here is correct, it follows that Jesus may have undertaken a Galilean village-to-village (or house-to-house) mission, in which houses, households, and sedentary followers of Jesus played a role similar to that which they played in Capernaum (Mark 6:1, 6, 56; 8:27; 9:30)."[77]

---

76 Gehring, p. 47.
77 Ibid., p. 43.

HOME-BASED OUTREACH

Christ's missional approach was to find a household willing to commit to his kingdom message. With this house as the base, Christ's followers attempted to reach the entire town and surrounding area.

Christ's original instructions were longer, but in Luke 9:1-9 and 10:1-11, we have compressed versions of those instructions. Luke 9 and 10 tell us that Jesus assigned the twelve and the seventy-two disciples to go from village to village and to enter homes, offering peace to the inhabitants.

Jesus sent them in pairs. He didn't want them to go alone. Each disciple needed a partner for fellowship, support, and ministry effectiveness. Jesus told them, "When you enter a house, first say, 'Peace to this house.' If a man of peace is there, your peace will rest on him; if not, it will return to you" (Luke 10: 5-6). When they found a "man of peace" (one desiring to find peace), they remained in that home, eating and drinking whatever was set before them. Living in the home was a key part of Christ's strategy.

The phrase "peace to this house" was also used in the literature of that time period and described someone who was qualified to receive peace. Jesus wanted his disciples to find people open to the gospel message. Their hospitality to receive Christ's messengers was the proof of their readiness to receive the message. A community, or new family, would be established in that house as a base of operations.

This peace message is actually the kingdom message, and those who receive Christ's kingdom were welcomed. Christ's charge to his disciples was to heal the sick and proclaim the presence of the reign of God, just as he did. Anyone who accepted the messengers and their peace greeting also accepted the message of the coming kingdom. So in one sense, God was going ahead of the disciples and establishing the household base, or beachhead, which made the way possible for the disciples to reach out and make disciples.

Who was supposed to receive the peace greeting? Most likely the disciples would win the head of the house. Then the conversion process would spread from there in ever widening circles, reaching its climax once the entire town had heard the kingdom message. Jewish households at that time period consisted of father, mother, children, and servants. In the Palestinian setting, only the head of the household would have been able to accept the greeting and offer an invitation to stay in the house.

Christ sent his disciples without food and clothing. Jesus told them, "Do not take a purse or bag or sandals . . . Stay in that house, eating and drinking whatever they give you, for the worker deserves his wages" (Luke 10:4, 7). The missionaries depended on the practical hospitality of the hosts, both for clothing and room and board. Roger Gehring writes, "The radical charge to enter into mission without equipment and outfitting, to renounce all belongings, and thus to be dependent on the hospitality of houses surely corresponds with the attitude and practice of Jesus."[78]

They were supposed to enter a home, convert the members of that particular household, and reach the other homes from a base location—rather than witnessing from house-to-house (Luke 10:7). Remaining in a house only makes sense if, beyond the initial proclamation of the kingdom message, the messengers stayed on to further nurture and establish a faith community.

In this way, a household would be converted to Christ and another house church would be formed. Jesus intended that the first house become a strategic base operation from which the other houses could be reached. Yet, the only way to do this was

78 Gehring, p. 53.

to have one strong base, one place to start, and from there the disciples could cover the entire area.

Today most scholars are in agreement that Christ's house church strategy was the starting point for church development after the resurrection. Christ's instructions in Luke 9 and 10 demonstrate that the pre-Easter house mission, as Jesus and his disciples practiced it, was the embryonic form of house-to-house outreach after Pentecost.[79]

The disciples in Acts followed Christ's strategy by reaching the family household structure *(oikos)* with the gospel message and then the entire city. One of the major reasons the early church was so effective was because they infiltrated the basic fabric of society—families living in homes. One problem with the church today is that people go to an event in a building, participate in various programs, but their lives don't change. Lohfink writes about Christ's house strategy,

> The houses into which the disciples entered were to become bases for the Jesus movement. A net of households into which eschatological peace had entered was to extend throughout the whole land. Everywhere in Israel there were to be people who were captivated by the reign of God and therefore trusted each other to share and care for one another. Thus there would be created a living basis that would support the disciples' work of proclamation.[80]

I've often taught that the early disciples after Pentecost naturally developed house groups because of Jethro's advice to Moses to establish groups of ten (Exodus 18), but it's far more likely that the disciples simply continued to follow the house-

---

79 Ibid., p. 58.
80 Lohfink, p. 167.

to-house strategy of their master given to them in Luke 9 and 10.

KINGDOM BUILDING

The kingdom Christ inaugurated didn't depend on ornate buildings or government structures. It was a spiritual kingdom that entered into the hearts and minds of families in the house setting. The Jews wanted a show of power and force, but Christ chose to make the change by transforming lives from the inside out. To do this, Christ utilized the most natural, practical, and reproducible structure to extend the kingdom message—house-to-house ministry.

Although Christ's message fueled the transformation, the vehicle was also important. Christ extended his kingdom message into the very fabric of the culture. In spite of the world's opposition, the gospel extended throughout the Roman Empire. The attraction was the changed lives of the followers and the formation of a new family based on love and servanthood.

Part 2

UNDERSTANDING EARLY CHURCH PRACTICES

Chapter Five

ECCLESIAL PRACTICE:
THE HOUSE IN THE NEW TESTAMENT CHURCH

When we hear the word *church* today, it sparks a wide array of images in our minds. For instance, I live in sunny southern California, and I can drive by *churches* like the Saddleback Church, Calvary Chapel, or the Crystal Cathedral. While you might not have such massive church images in your mind, most people do think in terms of *church* buildings, *church* meetings, and specific *church* days. Today when we read the New Testament, it's almost impossible to avoid these modern day images and experiences of *church*.

The fact is that the early Christians met primarily in the homes of individual members over a period of nearly three

e fourth century, when Constantine
silicas throughout the Roman Empire.
became so common that throughout
mention of a local church or of a
for worship or fellowship, is a reference
home. Men and women, ablaze with
to spread the gospel message from
20). House churches played an essential
role in the rapid growth and ultimate triumph of Christianity,
and it would be safe to say that the first three centuries belonged
to the house church movement.

THE FLAME SPREADS THROUGH HOUSES

At Pentecost, God baptized a new people with the Spirit of
God, and these believers spread the gospel throughout the
Mediterranean world, using the house church setting to expand
(Acts 1:13ff, 12:12). Scripture says, "And day by day continuing
with one mind in the temple, and breaking bread from house to
house, they were taking their meals together with gladness and
sincerely of heart, praising God and having favor with all the
people" (Acts 2:46; Acts 5:42).

Making its way through the Roman Empire, Christianity left
house churches in its wake. When Peter was released from
prison in Acts 12, he went to a house church in the home of
Mary. Scripture says, "He went to the house of Mary the mother
of John, also called Mark, where many people had gathered and
were praying" (Acts 12:12).

In Acts 3, John and Peter appear together. They traveled from
village to village, which implies from house-to-house, just as
Jesus instructed them in Luke 9:4-6 and 10:1-3. Peter also stayed
on in the house of Simon the tanner. We don't know how Simon

came to faith, but we do know that he extended hospitality to Peter and in doing so supported Peter's outreach in the area.

Then we see Peter following the example of Jesus to go house-to-house when he enters the house of Cornelius. Through the proclamation of the gospel, Cornelius and his entire household came to faith in Christ. Speaking about the conversion of Cornelius, Gehring writes,

> Through the peace greeting and the proclamation of the kingdom of God, the peace of God rests on the son of peace and his household (Luke 10:5-7; Matt 10:12-13). After this Peter is invited to stay a few days (compare Acts 10:48 with Luke 10:7). Many exegetes view Acts 10:1-48, among other things, as the story of the establishment of a house church and thus the history of the founding of the church in Caesarea.[81]

As the church moved out from Jerusalem, the gospel flame continued to spread through houses. The jailer's house at Philippi was an evangelistic center after his conversion (Acts 16:16-40). Jason's house at Thessalonica was used for evangelism (Acts 17:5).

After God opened up the heart of Lydia and her entire household was baptized, she invited missionaries into her home and offered them her hospitality for an undetermined period of time (Acts 16:14-15). Her house became a place where fellowship was enjoyed, a meeting place for worship, and a base of operations for Paul's mission.[82]

In Acts 18:7-8, we read that Crispus, the synagogue ruler, and his entire household believed in the Lord, and another house church was born.

---

81 Gehring, p. 108.
82 Ibid., p.131.

Philip welcomed visitors like Paul and his company to his house in Caesarea, as well as other Christians such as Agabus. In Acts 21:8-9, we learn that Philip was a homeowner in Caesarea. It was probably there that he earned the title *evangelist* (21:8). Philip ministered from Caesarea and targeted the surrounding area. Apart from being a mission headquarters, his house was possibly the meeting place for a house church.

Paul baptized Stephanas' household and apparently used their home "for the service of the saints" (1 Corinthians 16:15). Paul asks that greetings be given to "the brethren who are in Laodicea and also Nympha and the church that is in her house" (Colossians 4:15). Aquila and Priscilla maintained a church in their home wherever they lived, whether in Corinth or Rome (Acts 18:2ff, 26; Romans 16:5; 1 Corinthians 16:19; 2 Timothy 4:19).

In Corinth, Aquila worked as a tentmaker or leather craftsman and opened a shop there. Paul took advantage of this setting to develop evangelistic contacts. The citywide outreach spread out from this central point, and led to the formation of a house church with Paul and this couple as its nucleus.

Speaking of Aquila's house church, Gehring writes, "In such a room or in the shop itself about twenty believers could have assembled for a house church meeting."[83] One can imagine that some of the guests would have sat on tent canvases during house meetings. This couple offered themselves and their quarters for the Pauline mission outreach.

Paul's teaching to the church at Corinth assumes a small group setting where "each one" is participating. "When you come together, everyone has a hymn, or a word of instruction, a revelation, a tongue or an interpretation. All of these must be done for the strengthening of the church" (1 Corinthians 14:26).

---

83 Gehring, p. 136.

In Acts 18:7, we read that Paul moved into the house of Titius Justus, located next to the synagogue. Most likely this man was a God-fearer and wealthy. He was probably a strong leader in the early church because he owned a house that was large enough to provide Paul a venue for his evangelistic preaching ministry.

Many more house churches are assumed in Scripture. For example, it appears that traces of two additional house churches can be observed in Romans 16:14-15, "Greet Asyncritus, Phlegon, Hermes, Patrobas, Hermas and the brothers with them," and "Greet Philologus, Julia, Nereus and his sister, and Olympas and all the saints with them." These names represent the members of two house churches, to which an undetermined number of additional Christians belonged, some relatives, others slaves or emancipated slaves.[84]

Paul writes to a house church in his epistle to Philemon (verse 2). In Laodicea in Colossians 4:15, we see an example of a woman householder who was making her home available to the church (Laodicea was about nine miles from Colossae). She might have also been an overseer of this church. This was just one of the house churches of the local church in that area.

House-to-house ministry allowed the believers to challenge the social order of the day (1 Corinthians 7:20-24). They became witnesses—through their words, their lives, and their suffering. Because of the small size of house churches, it was possible to maintain a family-like atmosphere and practice brotherly love in a personal and effective way.

The early church followed the example of Jesus by establishing home churches throughout the Roman Empire. We've noticed this from households in Galilee, Jerusalem, and Jericho to those of Damascus (Acts 9:10-19), Joppa (Acts 9:43; 10:6, 17-18, 32), Caesarea (Acts 10:1-11:18; 21:18), Tyre (Acts 21:3-6), Philippi

---

84 Ibid., p. 145.

(Acts 16:15, 34, 40), Thessalonica (Acts 17:5-7), Ephesus (Acts 20:20), Troas (Acts 20:7-12), Corinth (Acts 18:3, 7-8), and Rome (Acts 28:16, 23, 30-31).

THE SIZE OF THE EARLY HOUSE CHURCHES

Church historians agree that these house churches could have rarely been more than fifteen or twenty people.[85] Once a house church grew larger than that, it usually multiplied by simply starting another house church nearby. If not, the growth immediately caused problems.[86] In other words, these houses were simply normal sized house structures. They weren't anything out of the ordinary.[87]

Since the houses of that time period differed from place to place, we can't be overly dogmatic about the size, shape, and pattern of each house. Gehring writes,

From an architectural point of view, the house offered certain strengths by providing space used in a variety of ways for missional outreach. To begin with, it should be pointed out that houses differ architecturally from one another. For the time period of the early Christian mission,

---

85 I recognize that some promote that the early house churches were not actually small groups but mid-sized groups of twenty-five to sixty. After researching this issue, my own conclusion is that few house churches were large enough to support a regular crowd of this many people. Granted, some house churches, like the upper room of Acts 2, had this capacity, but these were the exceptions rather than the rule.

86 Wolfgang Simson, *Houses That Changed the World* (Cornwall, UK: Authentic, 1998), pp. 40-41.

87 Ralph Neighbour says, "Excavations in Jerusalem reflect that only the wealthy had homes with second-floor 'Upper Rooms.' For the rest, residences would usually not accommodate more than ten to twelve persons," in *Where Do We Go from Here? A Guidebook for the Cell Group Church* (Houston, TX: Touch Publications, 2000), Kindle locations 578-579.

Palestinian, Greek, and Roman types of private houses come into question. They were easily adapted, and they provided Christians with a low-cost venue for assembly. With relatively little effort it was possible to establish a Christian presence in the everyday life of the ancient cities.[88]

Normally a house church met in a room, usually the dining room, of a private domestic house that was not changed or altered but was used for Christian purposes. The dining room, often in conjunction with the courtyard, provided space for teaching and preaching ministries, baptismal instruction, and other missional activities. It allowed the early Christians space for prayer meetings and the celebration of the Lord's Supper.

Osiek and Balch write, "Comparing archaeological digs of houses at that time, a typical house might have fit comfortably between 6 and 15 people. If the crowd spilled over into the gardens, more could have gathered."[89] Dining in Roman domestic life could last from the afternoon to late at night. Typically, nine to twenty guests were invited, arranged in a prescribed seating order.[90]

In the earliest years, perhaps for the first century and a half, there were probably no structural adaptations for Christian worship, but rather, believers adapted to the available structures. The size of the meeting space in the largest house available would limit the size of a worship group. When the group became too large, another home was founded in another location.[91]

---

88 Gehring, pp. 289-290.
89 Carolyn Osiek and David L. Balch, *Families in the New Testament World* (Louisville, KY: Westminster John Knox Press, 1997), p. 30
90 Wikipedia, accessed on Thursday, December 29, 2011 at http://en.wikipedia.org/wiki/Triclinium
91 Osiek and Balch, p. 33.

Excavations near Corinth uncovered an atrium house which contained a series of rooms surrounding a courtyard. It accommodated nine people on the couches placed along the walls, and in the courtyard there would have been room for several more. If all of the couches were removed, there would have been room for about twenty people.[92] Gehring says, "Because of the physical limitations of the *triclinium* [dining room] . . . these first Christian communities were small, family-like groups in which individual pastoral care, intimate personal relationships, and accountability to each other were possible."[93]

Although there is no archaeological evidence for Christian house churches in apartments of that early time period (called insula), it's probable that the earliest Christian meetings also took place in these rooms or apartments. "Those with Chloe" (1 Corinthians 1:11) may be an example. Paul's late night discourse in the third-story room at Troas (Acts 20:7-12) is probably another.[94] Osiek, MacDonald, and Tulloch conclude from their study of early house churches that, "Some Christian groups must certainly have met in more modest accommodations, even in some of the grimier apartment houses *(insulae)*." [95]

A very limited number of wealthy homes could fit up to one hundred twenty people (the upper room), but this was the exception rather than the rule. Banks writes,

The entertaining room in a moderately well-to-do household could hold around thirty people comfortably— perhaps half as many again in an emergency. The larger meeting in Troas, for example, was so large that Eutychus had to use the windowsill for a seat (Acts 20:9). A meeting

---

92 Gehring, p. 141.
93 Ibid., p. 290.
94 Osiek and Balch, p. 34.
95 Osiek,MacDonald, Tulloch, Kindle edition, p. 9.

of the "whole church" may have reached forty to forty-five people—if the meeting spilled over into the atrium then the number could have been greater, though no more than double that size—but many meetings may well have been smaller.[96]

The house churches were personal, friendly, and attractive to outsiders. Klauck writes, "One reason for the house church's powerful impact on its environment is found in the fact that it was not possible to grow beyond the parameters of a small group due to lack of space."[97]

WHAT DID THEY DO IN THE HOUSE GATHERINGS?

We read in the Gospel accounts that Jesus gathered his disciples in a house where he broke bread and shared wine to prepare the disciples for his death (e.g., Luke 22:7-38). The early church followed the example of Christ by breaking bread together. They shared a full meal while celebrating his death and resurrection (Acts 2:46; 1 Corinthians 11:20-26). William Barclay writes, "The Lord's supper began as a family meal or a meal of friends in a private house . . . It was there that the Lord's supper was born in the church. It was like the Jewish Passover which is a family festival at which the father and the head of the household is the celebrant."[98]

---

96 Banks, pp. 35-36.
97 Klauck, Hausgemeinde, as quoted in Roger W. Gehring, *House Church and Mission: The Importance of Household Structures in Early Christianity* (Peabody, MA: Hendrickson, 2004), p. 290.
98 William Barclay, *The Lord's supper* (SCM: London, 1967), p. 101 as quoted in Robert and Julia Banks, *The Church Comes Home: A New Base for Community and Mission* (Australia: Albatross Books, 1986), p. 59.

Everyone brought food, whether it was little or much, and shared it. They remembered that Christ's death on the cross brought salvation, and they looked forward to his second coming when they would enjoy the marriage feast of the Lamb.[99] Did they celebrate the Lord's Supper every time they met together? We don't know for certain, but apparently it was a frequent practice.

Beyond sharing the Lord's Supper together, the house church meetings were quite flexible. Paul wrote to the house church in Colossae, "Let the word of Christ dwell in you richly as you teach and admonish one another with all wisdom, and as you sing psalms, hymns and spiritual songs with gratitude in your hearts to God"(3:16). Paul wanted the house church believers to freely share, to encourage one another, and to rejoice in God's goodness. We don't see a rigid agenda. Rather, the meeting was a time to minister to one another and meet needs.

The writer of Hebrews exhorts the house church members to do something similar, "Let us hold unswervingly to the hope we profess, for he who promised is faithful. And let us consider how we may spur one another on toward love and good deeds. Let us not give up meeting together, as some are in the habit of doing, but let us encourage one another—and all the more as you see the Day approaching" (Hebrews 10:23-25). The Holy Spirit used each member as an instrument of edification.

The members enjoyed each other's presence, laughed together, and experienced rich fellowship. Robert Banks writes, "We find no suggestion that these meetings were conducted with the kind of solemnity and formality that surrounds most weekly Christian gatherings today."[100]

---

99 Lohfink, pp. 147-148.
100 Robert and Julia Banks, *The Church Comes Home: A New Base for Community and Mission* (Australia: Albatross Books, 1986), p. 39.

The early church saw itself as God's new family. Many of the house church meetings were also hosted and led by the same family. The intense love of these early Christ-followers permeated the meeting. They saw themselves as brothers and sisters and wanted to serve one another as Jesus served his own disciples. As mentioned earlier, the phrase one another appears more than fifty times in the New Testament. These phrases instructed the early believers on how to cultivate relationships among themselves.

Paul taught the early house churches that each member had an essential part according to his or her giftedness (1 Corinthians 12-14; Romans 12; Ephesians 4). He placed a high emphasis on participation because each person had a contribution to make. Paul addressed his letters to everyone in the house church because they were all ministers.

When writing to the Corinthian house church, Paul says, "When you come together, everyone has a hymn, or a word of instruction, a revelation, a tongue or an interpretation. All of these must be done for the strengthening of the church" (1 Corinthians 14:26). Paul assumed that they would energetically minister to each other. His concern was that "Everything should be done in a fitting and orderly way" (1 Corinthians 14:40). Ritva Williams writes, "The central activity of the ekklesia seems to have been a meal—the Lord's supper—followed by acts of prophecy, teaching, healing, and speaking in tongues (1 Corinthians 11-14)."[101]

We know that the early churches prayed together. After Peter was supernaturally released from prison, we read in Acts 12:12, "He went to the house of Mary the mother of John, also called Mark, where many people had gathered and were praying." They specifically were praying for Peter to be released from

---

101 Williams, p. 17.

prison, but we can assume that prayer characterized the house church meetings.

Most scholars agree that the early house churches emphasized the following elements:[102]

- Worship
- Practice of the spiritual gifts
- Teaching
- Prayer
- Fellowship
- Evangelism
- The Lord's Supper
- Baptism

Luke describes homes being used for prayer meetings (Acts 12:12); for an evening of Christian fellowship (Acts 21:7); for holy communion services (Acts 2:46); for a whole night of prayer, worship, and instruction (Acts 20:7); for impromptu evangelistic gatherings (Acts 16:32); for planned meetings to hear the gospel (Acts 10:22); for following up (Acts 18:26); and for organized instruction (Acts 5:42).[103]

Announcements and communication were also important activities in the early house churches. News from visitors, sending of letters from one city to another (e.g., Paul's letters, 2 and 3 John), warnings of persecution, and accounts of actual persecutions were all important types of information that passed through the house churches.[104]

The house churches also served as centers of social services for those members who were in need. Young widows and the

102 Gehring, p. 27.
103 Michael Green, *Evangelism in the Early Church* (Grand Rapids, MI: Eermans, 2003), Kindle locations 3776-3778.
104 Osiek, MacDonald, Tulloch, p. 14.

poorer family members looked to the house churches as a means of support. Apparently, there were some attempts by families to avoid their own responsibilities (1 Timothy 5:4, 5, 8, 16). [105]

INTIMATE CONNECTIONS

God chose a particular setting to share kingdom values. While the church exists apart from the structure it embodies, the home draws out the triune values of love, community, and family transformation. The early house church practices were linked and even determined by the venue—the what was determined by the where. Ralph Neighbour writes,

> There is a very important reason for the early church to be shaped in homes. It is in this location that values are shared. It may be possible to transmit information in a neutral building, but few values are implanted there. Value systems are ingrained through living together in a household. Something stirs deep within when life is shared between the young and old, the strong and the weak, the wise and the foolish. In the house groups, all participated and all were impacted by the values of the others as Christ lived within them. [106]

God crafted a reproducible strategy that depended on the believer's home property for the early meetings. Only those transformed by the gospel's message would risk opening their homes. Yet, all those who opened their homes exemplified God's love and power for their neighbors and friends to see and experience. In the process, many more were converted, and the early church continued to spread from house-to-house.

---

105 Ibid., p. 14.
106 Neighbour, *Where Do We Go from Here*, Kindle locations 584-585.

Chapter Six

ECCLESIAL LIFE:
THE OIKOS THAT MET IN
THE HOUSE

Arriving at a biblical theology requires imagining and envisioning what life was like for the first believers. It's one thing to acknowledge that the first Christians met in homes; it's quite another to visualize the culture inside those homes. What were the people like back then? How did their culture differ from our own? The inspired biblical writers didn't write Scripture in a vacuum. They had a particular culture and audience in mind when they wrote. The only way we can understand biblical teaching is to understand the context. Philip Esler points out,

> It is essential to note that these households were functioning families, containing family members and possibly slaves

and visiting clients, not just the shells of houses taken over for meetings of the congregation. As a result, the congregations were actually swept up into the social realities, the roles, values, and institutions, of particular families in the cities in which they were located.[107]

One of the major cultural gaps between then and now is the extended family, or the ancient *oikos* structure. For example, those who live in the Western, individualistic world have a hard time imagining the New Testament culture in which it was normal to live with parents, relatives, servants, and other workers. We are accustomed to living in nuclear families—father, mother, and children.

Yet, the ancient world didn't even have a way to express what we call the "nuclear family." We only find the word for extended family or *oikos*, which means household, house or family.

OIKOS RELATIONSHIPS

The word "house" (*oikia*) and "household" (*oikos*) play a prominent, if not dominant role in early church life. *Oikos* is found thirty-four times in Luke and twenty-five times in Acts. The head of the *oikos*, his extended family (wife and children), and slaves normally lived together in one domestic setting. Large *oikoi* also had farms that were usually tended by slaves, which were also the basic agricultural unit of the ancient economy.

---

107 Cf. H. Moxes, "What Is Family? Problems Constructing Early Christian Families," in *Constructing Early Christian Families: Family as Social Reality and Metaphor*, H. Moxes, ed. (London: Routledge, 1997), p. 25 as quoted in Andrew D. Clarke, *Serve the Community of the Church* (Grand Rapids, MI: Eerdmans, 2000), p. 162.

Scarcely anything determined daily life more than the *oikos* with its network of relationships. It was the prominent social structure of the day and included legal, economic, and biological implications. By belonging to a particular *oikos*, each person gained a sense of identity within the larger society. We can't overemphasize the significance of the oikos for the organization and expansion of the early Christian church.

The *oikos* structure served as each member's primary group of identification and was the immediate source of his or her ascribed honor. Ritva Williams writes, "Family solidarity, presenting a united front to the world outside the *oikos*, was regarded as crucial, and demanded uncompromising loyalty, respect, and obedience, first to one's parents and then to each other."[108] Because the early church evangelized through the natural *oikos* relationships, Christianity entered virtually all social classes.

OIKOS TRANSFORMATION

Christian house churches integrated a large diversity of individuals from a variety of backgrounds. Christ's death provided salvation for everyone, and the gospel message included the command to love one another and live in unity with each other. Williams writes, "Members of these Jesus groups were challenged to see themselves and behave toward one another as siblings, that is, children of a common Father in heaven, regardless of their ethnic, status, or gender differences."[109] However, this new order required a transformation from the cultural norms of the day, which divided people into strict roles and categories.

---

108 Williams, p. 24.
109 Ibid., p. 36.

The head and owner of the house, for example, wielded such a strong authoritative position that it was possible for unhealthy relationships to develop. Simply gathering in house churches didn't automatically transform the social structures of that day.[110] Most slaves were segregated in the typical Roman house.[111] When a house owner with slaves became a Christian and the house church assembled for worship and to celebrate the Lord's Supper, tension could easily develop between people of different social status and the call for Christ's new order, which declared that there was "neither slave nor free" (Galatians 3:28).

An example is Onesimus and Philemon. Onesimus, the slave of Philemon, became a brother in Christ. Paul makes it clear that Philemon was no longer merely the earthly master but also an equal who could potentially be even exhorted by Onesimus (Philemon 8-19). Karl Sandnes writes,

Paul is struggling to express the new identity of Onesimus in relation to his master. First he denies that "slave" is an appropriate word for this new relationship. Onesimus has become the brother of Philemon in every way. Both Philemon and Onesimus have a new status ascribed to them. They both owe the Christian faith to Paul, the apostle of Christ . . . In the Lord, the master and his slave have entered a new relationship to God (vv. 3-4) on an equal basis, and also a new relationship to each other. They are now equal brothers.[112]

In Romans 16:3-15, the list of house churches and groups shows the immense diversity also within a network of home-

---

110 Gehring, p. 295.
111 Williams, p. 27.
112 Karl Olav Sandnes, "Equality within Patriarchal Structures," in *Constructing Early Christian Families*, Halvor Moxnes, ed. (London: Routledge, 1997), p. 157.

based groups in the same city. Over half the names are Latin (e.g. Urbanus) or Greek (e.g. Hermes), suggesting that Gentiles outnumbered Jews (e.g. Herodion, Mary). Some member's names suggest they originally came from as far away as Persia (e.g. Persis) and Africa (e.g. Rufus). Moreover, several names are common slave names (e.g. Ampliatus, Julia, Urbanus). There must have been practical challenges in creating a loving, united, faith community with such socioeconomic and cultural diversity.

The transforming gospel message proclaimed a new family of God, in which each member was a child of God with full kingdom rights. Paul says to the house churches in Galatia,

> You are all sons of God through faith in Christ Jesus, for all of you who were baptized into Christ have clothed yourselves with Christ. There is neither Jew nor Greek, slave nor free, male nor female, for you are all one in Christ Jesus. If you belong to Christ, then you are Abraham's seed, and heirs according to the promise (Galatians 3:26-29).

In Jesus, rigid societal distinctions ceased to exist. In the small, family-like setting of the house church, individuals from different social backgrounds were united into one new community, but this wasn't always easy. Yet, by the power of God, the house churches did display a new, loving order of humility and service. The way Christians lived in community with one another, in spite of their social differences, made a profound impact.

OIKOS OUTREACH

As Jesus transformed people, they behaved differently within their oikos relationships. Husbands loved wives, slaves were treated with dignity, married partners submitted to one another,

and love reigned supreme. Friends and neighbors were drawn
to this new transformed community. Hellerman writes,

> The movement attracted people because of the Christians'
> behavior toward one another and toward those outside the
> church. Yes, Christian beliefs were appealing . . . The
> ancient church was a strong-group family of surrogate
> siblings who lived out their belief system in a practical and
> winsome way. [113]

The main evangelistic outreach was the attractiveness of the
community life that the early believers projected. People could
see the changes up close as community life was lived out in the
open.

The attractiveness of this new, called out society spread
throughout the Mediterranean world. When people noticed
how lives were changed and how the believers bonded together,
they believed the gospel message. Christians would gather
together in homes to instruct one another, study, pray, and use
their spiritual gifts. Their pagan neighbors witnessed that Christ
had established a new order—one based upon love and caring
relationships.[114] Osiek and Balch write,

> It is also possible but not likely that in a domus [large
> house], the neighbors may not have known what was taking
> place. But certainly in the case of meetings held in an insula
> [apartment], there could have been no question of secrecy,
> for everyone in the building must have known everyone
> else's business. 1 Corinthians 14:23 seems to suggest that
> outsiders regularly were invited or perhaps even wandered
> into Christian meetings. It would be a mistake, therefore,

---

113 Hellerman, p. 106.
114 Ray Stedman, *Body Life* (Glendale, CA: Regal Books, 1972), 108.

to envision every Christian gathering at this time in a spacious private house, or even operating with full privacy.[115]

God designed the early house churches to be a practical demonstration of his power to transform the social order. House churches were a training ground for Christian community and an example of living for Christ. Gehring writes:

> The ancient oikos with its network of relationships provided a very favorable opportunity for evangelistic contacts. In this setting it would have been quite natural to pass on the Christian message from person to person (from householder to householder, from slave to slave, etc.). For example, an invitation to a meal in the home would have created an opportunity to cultivate contacts and deepen relationships. The first Christians certainly would have engaged in conversations about the faith in their homes— in a certain sense, evangelism from house to house.[116]

The extended family was the core of the congregation, which explains the rapid expansion of the Christian movement.[117] Gerhard Lohfink writes, "The natural family, which constituted the central focus of the several houses, was opened and joined into a broader context: the new family of the community."[118]

Paul the apostle, more than anyone else, was responsible for taking the Christian message from the world of Judaism to the Greco-Roman world. Paul not only had to work out strategies for evangelism in the cities he visited but also strategies to

---

115 Osiek and Balch, pp. 34-35.
116 Gehring, p. 92.
117 Ibid., p. 193.
118 Lohfink, p., 263

mature his converts and to develop leaders. Scripture tells us that Paul did these things in houses (Acts 20:20).

Paul would normally convert homeowners, so that believers would be able to meet together and build one another up in the faith. The homes of these converts provided a meeting place and beachhead for organizing church life. Paul depended on the hospitality of these converts, and they were essential to his mission.

He affirmed the leadership of those responsible for each group and continued to supervise them by personal visits, sending delegates, and through letters. Paul acted quickly and decisively whenever he noticed doctrinal problems.

Paul's strategy is evident in Corinth in the household of Stephanas. As the head of the home, he was baptized along with his *oikos* (1 Corinthians 1:16). Paul calls his household the first converts of Achaia (1 Corinthians 16:15-16). This means that Paul considered this house to have embraced the Christian faith through the conversion of Stephanas. The entire household of Stephanas devoted itself to ministering to the church.

According to Acts 16:15, a similar event took place in Lydia's house. Lydia, probably a widow continuing her husband's business, was converted with her household: "When she and her household were baptized she urged us, saying, 'If you have judged me to be faithful to the Lord, come and stay at my home.'" Michael Green writes,

> The household proved the crucial medium for evangelism within natural groupings, whatever member of the family was first won to the faith. It was preferable, of course, that the father be converted first, for then he would bring over the whole family with him. This is what happened in the case of Cornelius, when he contemplated a change of superstition. He gathered together his blood relatives, his slaves and his friends, and together they heard the preaching

of Peter . . . The same happened in the case of Lydia, a textile saleswoman from Thyatira operating for the time being in Philippi. Her whole household (no doubt largely slaves, together with some freedmen, but without spouse and children in this case, as she seems to have been unmarried) was baptized. So also was the household of the Philippian jailer when he professed faith. It was the natural thing.[119]

Conversion, however, did not always take place in households. Sometimes only the husband converted, sometimes only the wife. The New Testament provides little information about the intra-familial tensions caused by the conversion of individuals. The New Testament writers clearly tell us, however, that problems existed in marriages in which only one of the two was a Christian, and in households where a slave was a believer (1 Corinthians 7:10-16).[120]

URBAN MINISTRY

Many believers were added to the church during the apostolic period (35-120 AD). Missiologist Robert T. Glover writes, "On the basis of all the data available, it has been estimated that by the close of the apostolic period the total number of Christian disciples had reached half a million."[121]

Although all historians believe that early Christianity grew substantially, not all believe it happened so quickly. For example, Rodney Stark, writing as a sociologist, estimates that the

---

119 Green, Kindle locations 3652-3658.
120 Sandnes, *Constructing Early Christian Families*, p.154.
121 As quoted by Patzia, p. 142.

Christian growth was much lower at the end of the apostolic period, but by 350 AD Christians numbered "many millions."[122]

Either way, the church grew over time and part of the explosive growth of Christianity happened because it became an urban movement. As Wayne Meeks writes, "Within a decade of the crucifixion of Jesus, the village culture of Palestine had been left far behind, and the Greco-Roman city became the dominant environment of the Christian movement."[123]

House church networks infiltrated the large urban centers of Rome and continued to expand and grow. Osiek and Balch say, "It must be kept in mind that the vast majority of people, perhaps as many as ninety percent in larger cities, lived in the much more constricted quarters of the *insula* or in apartments of one or two rooms crowded above or behind shops."[124] At the height of its population, Rome might have had one million inhabitants. House churches—or more precisely, apartment churches—spread throughout these dense cities, and Christ transformed the inhabitants.

Because the Roman Empire conquered many nations, about two million slaves lived in the region. Slavery in the Mediterranean world was neither race-specific nor racist. Most of the slaves worked as domestic and personal servants.[125]

The Greco-Roman cities were usually filthy and overpopulated. Homelessness, poverty, and violent ethnic strife were common. The cities were a melting pot of ethnic diversity.[126] In addition to the physical misery, Greco-Roman cities suffered from social

---

122 Rodney Stark, *Cities of God* (New York: Harper Collins 2009), Kindle edition, p. 64.

123 Wayne Meeks, *First Urban Christians: The Social World of the Apostle Paul* (New Haven, CT: Yale University Press, 1983), p. 11, as quoted in Rodney Stark, *The Rise of Christianity* (San Francisco, CA: HarperSanFrancisco, 1997), p. 129.

124 Osiek and Balch, p. 31.

125 Williams, p. 25.

126 Stark, *Cities of God*, pp. 28-29.

chaos, high mortality rates, and a constant influx of immigrants. The constant arrival of newcomers reflected an extraordinary ethnic diversity. However, the diverse groups did not assimilate, but created and sustained their own separated enclaves— resulting in frequent turf battles and sometimes all-out riots.

With the exception of Rome, the cities were small and many people suffered from living a too-intimate, insufficiently private life.[127] Reta Finger writes,

> Cities demanded a high level of communal sharing. From the narrow streets, even narrower alleys led into courtyards . . . The basic residential unit was a courtyard around which one or more rows of houses adjoined each other. Most of the courtyards were owned jointly by several families, or by a large extended family.[128]

Life for most was difficult with few possessions. Some houses were larger, but many families lived in a single room. It was common for an extended family to share a house, dividing the rooms into smaller family units. Much of the baking was done outside and the dining room was the largest room in the house.[129]

Although these cities were not as large as cities today, they were often more densely populated. While only Rome and Alexandria had more than one hundred fifty thousand people, many cities had fewer than fifty thousand. Yet these cities covered very small areas and as a result, people were packed together.

Antioch had a population of about one hundred thousand, but it was only two miles long and one mile wide. This means

---

127 Ibid., pp. 28-29,.
128 Finger, p. 121.
129 Ibid., pp. 121-122.

that 78.2 people lived per acre, but this is not including space devoted to temples, public buildings, and streets. The density would increase to one hundred thirty people per acre if these other spaces were added. This is a greater density than modern-day Calcutta.[130]

Even though these statistics for Antioch seem amazing, Rome was far more crowded. It is estimated that between two hundred to three hundred persons packed into a square acre. This would be similar to a crowded hot beach on today's most popular holiday of the year with people packed into every available space.[131]

In spite of the undesirable conditions, rent was expensive, especially in Rome. It's estimated that an average room cost forty *denarii* a month. Since an average worker only made about one *denarius* per day, families had to share space and gather money into one common purse.

Most apartment blocks were made with timber and mud brick, making them prone to fire and collapse. The upper floors were without heat or running water and only sometimes had lavatories. Granted, most cities did set aside space for gardens, baths, and city squares.[132] Wayne Meeks writes,

> Privacy was rare in such small houses in a dense area. For instance, in Rome, most people lived in small apartments called *insulae*, in poor conditions with a high rental fee. Most people lived on streets and sidewalks. The house was for sleeping and storing one's belongings. Privacy was not

---

130 Stark, *Cities of God,* p. 27.
131 Ibid., pp. 26-27.
132 Reta Halteman Finger, *Roman House Churches for Today: A Practical Guide for Small Groups* (Grand Rapids, MI: Eerdmans, 2007), Kindle locations 345-349.

possible for the ordinary person. Life happened in front of the neighbors.[133]

It's crucial to understand that in the ancient world, life happened in front of the neighbors. In our privatized world, it's hard to imagine what the early church experienced. The members of the house offered love and hope in the midst of misery. People could envision a better way of life, and these meetings helped make city life more tolerable. In this dense, public milieu, there were many opportunities to share the gospel. The apostle Paul says he preached publicly and from house-to-house (Acts 19:8-12; 20:20).

Public preaching brought many house churches into existence, but then the *oikos* web structure through house-to-house ministry sustained the growth. House meeting not only took care of the converts, but also became outposts to attract people in the neighborhood.

The urban outreach of the early believers brought them in contact with people of every social class. Osiek and Balch write,

Christianity's profile was not that of a highly selective, educated, or high-status group. On the contrary, while there were some higher-status members, probably all of whom functioned as patrons of house churches and later of the organized local church, the church encouraged and welcomed those of modest status and offered them not an esoteric and sophisticated system of beliefs, but one that was freely taught to all and which all could comprehend.[134]

---

133 Wayne Meeks, *The First Urban Christians: The Social World of the Apostle Paul* (New Haven, CT: Yale University Press, 1983), p. 29, as quoted in Hae Gyue Kim, *Biblical Foundations for the Cell-Based Churches Applied to the Urban Context of Seoul, Korea* (Pasadena, CA: Fuller Theological Seminary, 2003), p. 89.
134 Osiek and Balch, p. 162.

In fact, often early Christianity spread to the lower classes in the urban milieu. Paul says to the Corinthians that not many were wise or of high status, but a few were. Christians were not, of course, immune to their culture, but an integral part of it. Gehring writes,

> The house churches corresponded closely with the ancient society around them, as the ancient *oikos* reflected the social order of that time (status, station, rank, position, class, profession), composed of almost all the different social strata. As a result, the composition of the early Christian movement was not limited to specific groups in the population. Christians were therefore positioned to reach all levels of society with the gospel. . . . The integration of the house church within the *oikos* had a positive effect not only for the spread of the gospel; it also enabled continuity, duration, and tradition. With the integration into *oikos* infrastructures, the Christian church became capable of long-term survival and was given the potential to transition from one generation to the next.[135]

Osiek and Balch note, "It is the middle levels (but not as a middle class), between the elites and those of no status at all, that most early Christians are to be located."[136] Christ followers transformed by the Gospel challenged the surrounding culture bound by societal distinctions.

---

135 Gehring, p. 292.
136 Osiek and Balch, p. 97.

CHRISTIANITY NEXT DOOR

God used the ancient *oikos* to extend the gospel throughout the Roman Empire. The early believers modeled transformed lives and distinct values that often ran counter-culture to the rest of society. Yet, in these crowded, urban environments, people were able to see Christianity up close. They heard and saw the testimonies of those transformed by the gospel, and then they desired to experience Christ for themselves. Rather than separating the believers from their own culture, God transformed people living with the household structure of the day.

However, to keep the young movement from burning itself out, God provided grassroots leadership to guide the movement and keep it on course.

Chapter Seven

ECCLESIAL LEADERSHIP:

DEVELOPING MINISTERS FROM THE HOUSE STRUCTURE

When we think about church leadership, we typically project our current experience on the leadership passages of Scripture. For example, Peter exhorts elders to willingly shepherd God's flock, not in a controlling way, but in humility and the fear of God, knowing that a heavenly rewards awaits those who shepherd faithfully (1 Peter 5:1-11).

Someone reading this passage from a Baptist background might imagine that Peter had Baptist polity in mind and could easily forget who Peter was talking to and what leadership roles actually existed in the first century. Presbyterians, on the other hand, have another view of an elder's authority and will probably study 1 Peter 5 while wearing twenty-first century reading glasses.

In other words, we all have the tendency to automatically interject our own experiences on the Bible, rather than beginning with first century principles and applying those principles to the twenty-first century.

But what would happen if we started with the first century worldview and moved forward over time to our current circumstances? What if we allowed the patterns back then to critique and shape what we do today? If we are willing to do this, the biblical narrative will instruct and critique our own leadership models.

So how did leadership emerge in the early church? What key characteristics did Paul and the other New Testament writers look for?

APOSTOLIC OVERSIGHT

Jesus trained the first church leaders—his very own disciples. In Acts 6:2, Scripture says, "So the Twelve gathered all the disciples together and said, 'It would not be right for us to neglect the ministry of the word of God in order to wait on tables.'"

Among the twelve, Peter maintained a position of preeminence (Acts 1-12; Galatians 1:18). Not only was Peter the leader of the house church in the upper room, he also led the Jerusalem church. Peter probably led the team of apostles in Acts 6, when the twelve asked the multitude to find seven leaders. Yet we no longer hear about Peter after the first council in Jerusalem (Acts 15). Most likely he had to leave the leadership team in Jerusalem because of persecution.[137]

---

137 Gehring, p. 100.

After Peter disappeared, the leadership mantle passed over to James, the Lord's brother. James emerged to become head elder of the Jerusalem church, as we can see in the Jerusalem council in Acts 15:13, where he assumes authority and gives the final pronouncement to the question of grace versus following law.[138]

Although Paul was not among the twelve, Jesus did appear to him personally and gave him an apostolic commission (1 Corinthians 15:1-11; Acts 9:1-19). Paul's apostolic ministry mainly focused on the Gentile world while Peter and James concentrated on the Jewish converts (Galatians 2:7-8). Paul planted house churches throughout the Roman world, developed leadership from his converts, and then mentored the new leaders as Christianity continued to spread. For example after planting churches throughout the empire, Paul says to his team, "Let us go back and visit the brothers in all the towns where we preached the word of the Lord and see how they are doing. . . . He went through Syria and Cilicia, strengthening the churches" (Acts 15:36, 41).

Because of the growth of the early church, the need for leadership expanded rapidly. One of the first leadership shortages occurs in Acts 6, where we see the widows of the Grecian Jews being overlooked in the daily distribution of food. The apostles asked the disciples to choose leaders from among themselves. Most likely the disciples chose seven leaders from those with leadership ability already proven in the house church structure.[139]

The early apostles provided the overarching leadership but depended on the house church leaders to shepherd and care for the rest of God's church. The authors of *Home Groups and House Churches* write,

---

138 Patzia, Kindle edition, p. 155.
139 Gehring, p. 97.

In the apostolic period, it was the apostles who gave general guidance to the life of the house churches; the original eleven under the leadership of James in Judea and Paul in the Gentile world with Peter moving somewhat in both worlds. There was a certain authority which emanated from their ministries. Otherwise, leadership in the churches centered in the host and/or leader of the house church. A variety of leadership roles and functions existed in the various house congregations: bishops (overseers), pastors, elders, prophets, teachers, and deacons. There may have been some distinction among the functions of bishops, or elders, and deacons; but these roles were not formalized in a definitive way in the New Testament era.[140]

INCUBATING LEADERS IN THE HOUSE CHURCH STRUCTURE

The early house churches were the incubators for leadership. Often the person who opened his or her home would assume the leadership role. William Lane concludes,

The host who possessed the resources and initiative to invite the church into his or her home assumed major leadership responsibilities deriving from the patronage offered. These included important administrative tasks, such as the provision of the common meals of the community, the extension of hospitality to traveling missionaries and other Christians, the representation of the community outside the domestic setting, in addition to

---

140 Hadaway, DuBose, Wright, p. 68.

pastoral oversight and governance . . . those who acted as patrons were in some sense also involved in governance of the community.[141]

Many are amazed at how quickly Paul developed leadership in the early church. In Paul's church plants, we don't see formal leadership structures. Why? Because Paul used the *oikos* structure to develop leadership naturally. Gehring writes, "For the congregation that met in a house, a leadership structure was already in place from the very beginning, built into the social infrastructure of the ancient *oikos* in advance."[142]

We don't read about the official installation of church leaders because it really wasn't necessary as the homeowners opened their homes. Leaders emerged from within the house church setting. Granted, these leaders had to be accepted by the house church members and by Paul.[143] Giles writes,

An example of how such a house-church might begin is given in Acts 17:1-9, where we read about the first Christians at Thessalonica who found in Jason's home a center for their assembling. The 'head' of such a household would naturally be recognized as having oversight of the new church. His social standing would give him pre-eminence in the group; his close association with the apostle who founded the church and sought his assistance would add to this. And as time passed, the fact that he was the first (or

---

141 W.L. Lane, "Social Perspectives of Roman Christianity during the Formative Years from Nero to Nerva: Romans, Hebrews, 1 Clement," pp. 211-212, as quoted in Andrew D. Clarke, *Serve the Community of the Church* (Grand Rapids, MI: Eerdmans, 2000), p. 164.
142 Gehring, p. 201.
143 Ibid., p. 298.

one of the first) converts would further enhance his position in the group.[144]

Often these house owners had their *oikos* built in and the gospel penetrated the entire household. The natural leadership produced rapid growth and reproduction. I've also noticed this same dynamic in most growing cell churches around the world. Leaders are developed naturally from within the cell structure and eventually become leaders because of their faithfulness and fruitfulness in ministry.

Those leaders who emerged from the households were only later given titles. In 1 Thessalonians 5:12-13, Paul says, "Now we ask you, brothers, to respect those who work hard among you, who are over you in the Lord and who admonish you. Hold them in the highest regard in love because of their work." Paul is talking about house church leaders, but he didn't feel it was worth mentioning their exact title. In other words, they developed organically within the house church structure.[145]

Harry Maier argues persuasively that we ought to look to the household, the social setting in which the early churches met to derive the origins of the leadership structures.[146] Granted, many others were raised up as house church leaders besides the home owners themselves, but it is important to know that often the hosts doubled as leaders of the house churches.

In 1 Corinthians 16:15-16, Paul says, "You know that the household of Stephanas were the first converts in Achaia, and they have devoted themselves to the service of the saints. I urge

144 Kevin Giles, *Patterns of Ministry among the First Christians* (Melbourne, Australia: Collins Dove, 1989), p. 31.
145 Gehring, p. 198.
146 Harry O. Maier, *The Social Setting of the Ministry as Selected in the Writings of Hermas, Clement and Ignatius* (Dissertations SRI; Waterloo, ON: Wilfrid Laurier University Press, 1991), pp., 4, 148-53, 155-56, 187.

you, brothers, to submit to such as these and to everyone who joins in the work, and labors at it." Paul challenged the Corinthians to submit to Stephanas and to those who work hard for the church. Stephanas made his home available to the believers and provided care for the group. Arthur G. Patzia writes,

Recently, certain scholars have connected local congregational leadership to the head of the household where the church met. Such could be the case with Stephanas as well as with Priscilla and Aquila (Romans 16:3-5; 1 Corinthians 16:19) and Philemon and Apphia (Philemon vv. 1-2). [147]

The writers of *Home Cell Groups and House Churches* say,

What seems clear in the New Testament is that next to the apostles themselves, the house church leaders were the most important in terms of the ongoing life of the church. Since there was no actual distinction between clergy and laity in the New Testament and since all leaders had other vocations, it is difficult to distinguish between "minister types" (Priscilla and Aquila) and "lay types" (Philemon and Nympha). No doubt some of the house church leaders were bishops and elders, but certainly not all of them appear to have been. [148]

In the New Testament, we don't find an exact prescriptive of church government because leadership developed naturally and spontaneously. Gehring says, "Nowhere in the New

---

147 Arthur Patzia, *The Emergence of the Church: Context, Growth, Leadership & Worship* (Downer's Grove, IL: InterVarsity, 2001), pp. 160-161.
148 Hadaway, DuBose, Wright, p. 69.

Testament do we find a picture closely resembling any of the fully developed systems of today. It is likely that in those days church government was not very highly developed, indeed, that local congregations were rather loosely knit groups."[149] Gilbert Bilezikian writes,

Whatever leadership structures existed in the early churches, they were inconspicuous, discreet, self-effacing, and flexible. They seem to have adapted their activities and visibility to local circumstances and needs. Clearly evident is a concern not to preempt congregational initiative and involvement. The leadership of New Testament churches seems to stand on the sidelines, ready to intervene only in situations of necessity. They are invisible servants, whose role is to equip the body. [150]

Those early house meetings encouraged everyone to participate. As the Spirit of God ministered through each member and each one served one another, God would develop certain ones to serve in a leadership role.

Paul's perception of Christian leadership came from his understanding of the church's nature. He viewed the church as the body of Christ and that all church roles were under the authority of Christ, the head of the church.[151] Everyone needed to give allegiance to the living head, while faithfully serving and loving one another.

---

149 Millard Erickson, *Christian Theology* (Grand Rapids, MI: Baker, 1998), p. 1094.
150 Bilezikian, p. 97.
151 Hae Gyue Kim, *Biblical Foundations for the Cell-Based Churches Applied to the Urban Context of Seoul, Korea* (Pasadena, CA: Fuller Theological Seminary, 2003), p. 101.

THE PRIESTHOOD OF BELIEVERS OPERATING THROUGH THE SPIRITUAL GIFTS

The Holy Spirit developed and guided early church leadership. Church ministry was fluid and dynamic. Members were encouraged to experience their spiritual gifts for the common good of the body, and leaders operated as gifted men and women (Romans 12:6-8; 1 Corinthians 12:8-10, 27-28).

The priesthood of all believers was the norm in the early church, and for this reason the early church spread rapidly. Gilbert Bilezikian writes,

In a few decades, the early church movement spread like wildfire through the ancient world. One of the secrets for this rapid expansion was total lay involvement in the ministries of the local churches . . . The book of Acts and most of the New Testament letters are permeated with the euphoria and the vitality of churches where everyone was involved in body life and ministry. Under normal circumstances, therefore, the apostle Paul was more interested in encouraging Christian folks to minister to each other and together than in setting up orders of hierarchy for their governance.[152]

Dependence on the Spirit of God through the gifts of the Spirit shaped the direction of the early church. The spiritual gifts mentioned in 1 Corinthians 12-14, Romans 12:3-8, Ephesians 4:7-12, and 1 Peter 4:8-11 were written to those participating in house churches. Because God gave gifts to each individual within the community, the focus was strongly

---

152 Bilezikian, p. 99.

egalitarian. Everyone participated in the building up of Christ's body.[153]

Paul expected church leadership to develop according to spiritual giftedness and that ultimately the Holy Spirit would set each member in the body according to his will and purpose (1 Corinthians 12:11). The early church believed that the Spirit was given to all believers and was actively working through each member (Romans 12:11; 1 Corinthians 2:4, 12:7;12-13; Galatians 3:5; 5:18, 22; 1 Thessalonians 5:19-21).[154]

God did gift certain individuals to lead his church as we can see in Ephesians 4:7-12. Many have called this the five-fold ministry, although it's probably more accurate to call it the four-fold ministry, since pastor-teacher is often considered one role. Gifted leaders included:

- Apostles: The Twelve (Luke 6:13-16), plus Matthias (Acts 1:24-26), Paul (Galatians 1:1), Barnabas (Acts 14:14), Andronicus and Junias (Romans 16:7)
- Prophets: The company from Jerusalem (Acts 11:27-28), Agabus (Acts 21:10-11), Judas and Silas (Acts 15:32) and the daughters of Philip (Acts 21:9)
- Evangelists: Philip's daughters (Acts 21:9)
- Pastor-teachers (1 Timothy 3:1-3, 5:17; Titus 1:5, 7, 9)

The gifted leaders mentioned in Ephesians were specifically equipped to prepare the body of Christ to minister more

---

153 Banks, 1994, p. 148.
154 Patzia, pp. 153-154.

effectively. In other words, God equipped these men and women to mobilize the church for service.[155]

Paul's main point in Ephesians is equipping the saints for ministry. The specific purpose of gifted men and women is to equip the church for growth and expansion. The focus is not on the gifted person, but on his or her ministry to equip the body of Christ so that the body of Christ would be built up and mobilized for service. Whatever gift God distributes to a particular person, his or her main role is to equip God's people, so he or she can minister more effectively.

Paul also mentions some twenty gifts (not just four or five) and wants his readers to know that each house church member needed to minister according to his or her giftedness (1 Corinthians 12-14; Romans 12; Ephesians 4:11-12; 1 Peter 4:8-11). And whether recognized formally or not, each member had an important part to play in the body of Christ (1 Corinthians 12:12-26). The spiritual gifts were to build up the body of Christ in unity and maturity.

WOMEN IN CHURCH LEADERSHIP

The New Testament portrays women as full participants in the church. Peter reminded the hearers on the day of Pentecost,

> These men are not drunk, as you suppose. It's only nine in the morning! No, this is what was spoken by the prophet Joel: "In the last days, God says, I will pour out my Spirit

---

155 Sadly, some present day teachers have over emphasized the five-fold ministry by teaching that every church (large or small) must identify all four or five offices and that without all of these leadership gifts functioning, the local church is doomed to failure. Some of these teachers also infer that only the ones who have an evangelist gift should be evangelizing; only the ones with a pastoral gift should shepherd the local church; and only those who have the gift of apostle should oversee church plants.

on all people. Your sons and daughters will prophesy, your young men will see visions, your old men will dream dreams. Even on my servants, both men and women, I will pour out my Spirit in those days, and they will prophesy" (Acts 2:15-18).

Your sons and daughters will prophesy and dream dreams. Paul says something similar in Galatians 3:28, "There is neither Jew nor Greek, slave nor free, male nor female, for you are all one in Christ Jesus." Speaking of this text, Gordon Fee writes,

Indeed, on the basis of this text and its place in the argument of Galatians—where socialized distinctions between people in their relationship to God have been overcome by Christ and the Spirit—one must argue that the new creation has brought in the time when the Spirit's gifting (the Spirit who is responsible for ushering in the new order) should precede roles and structures, which are on a carryover from the old order that is passing away. [156]

This new era or new creation is focused on the *charisma* of the Spirit working through both male and females. The gifts of the Spirit are not gender or role specific. In Romans 12:8, where Paul talks about the gift of leadership, the pronoun "your" is genderless. Leadership was given to both men and women.

Paul and the other New Testament writers demonstrate the significant role that women played in the New Testament church. Approximately one-fourth of Paul's co-workers are women. If Nympha, mentioned in Colossians, is added, and Lydia, in Acts, there are a total of twelve women who Paul

---

[156] Gordon Fee, "Male and Female in the New Creation," in *Discovering Biblical Equality,* Ronald W. Pierce and Rebecca Merrill Goothuis, general eds. (Downers Grove, ILL: InterVarsity Press, 2004), p. 185.

mentions prominently: Euodia, Julia, Junias, Lydia, Mary, Nympha, Persis, Phoebe, Priscilla, Syntyche, Tryphena, and Tryphosa.[157]

Seven of them were instrumental in the house church movement in Rome: Priscilla (Romans 16:3), Mary (Romans 16:6), Junias (Romans 16:7), Tryphena, Tryphosa, Persis (Romans 16:12) and Julia (Romans 16:15).

Arthur Patzia writes, "The overall impression from Luke's and Paul's perspective is that women played a significant role in the life, ministry, and leadership of the early church."[158] Paul treated women with equal dignity and valued their contribution to the ministry of the gospel. Paul wanted to break down the barriers that existed between ethnic groups and gender classes. His desire was to see the church implement unity among males and females.[159]

As mentioned earlier, various women were house church hosts and leaders. Mary the mother of John Mark appears to have been a leader of one of the early Christian groups, her house being used for church meetings (Acts 12:12); Lydia's household served as a gathering place for the early believers in Philippi (Acts 16:12-15, 40); in Thessalonica (Acts 17:4) several "leading women" responded to the gospel; as did other Greek women in Berea (Acts 17:12).

The fact that Nympha hosted one of the house churches shows that women were allowed positions of authority and leadership. Nympha would have been a person of social standing and wealth who had a large home. She was probably a widow who owned land or managed a business and was the "head" of

---

157 Gehring, p. 211.

158 Patzia, p. 178.

159 Stanley J. Grenz, Denise Muir Kjesbo, *Women in the Church: A Biblical Theology of Women in Ministry* (Downers Grove, IL: InterVarsity, 1995), Kindle locations 1180-1183.

an extended family including blood relations, employees, and slaves.[160]

Paul says about Phoebe, "I commend to you our sister Phoebe, a servant of the church in Cenchrea. I ask you to receive her in the Lord in a way worthy of the saints and to give her any help she may need from you, for she has been a great help to many people, including me" (Romans 16:1-2). Phoebe made her own house available to the congregation as a meeting place, serving as hostess. She probably took over responsibilities of the absent housefather. It could be that Phoebe had a teaching ministry in the house church in Cenchrea and delivered the letter to the Romans but also read and explained it to the house churches in Rome.[161] Osiek, MacDonald, and Tulloch have studied the women's place in the early house churches and conclude,

> To step into a Christian house church was to step into a women's world. This was true even when the leader of the assembly was male. Further, it can be established that women, probably for the most part widows who had autonomous administration of their own households, hosted house churches of the early Christian movement.[162]

In the early church, women were active evangelists, coworkers, patrons, and even apostles. It is virtually certain that Paul refers to the woman Junia as an apostle in Romans 16:7. Some Bibles translate this passage as referring to the male apostle "Junias."

However, Eldon Jay Epp is an eminent New Testament scholar who has recently done the definitive study on Romans

---

160 Kevin Giles, *What on Earth is the Church? An Exploration in New Testament Theology* (Downers Grove, IL: InterVarsity, 1995), p. 130.
161 Gehring, p. 219.
162 Osiek, MacDonald, Tulloch, Kindle edition, p. 163.

16:7 in his book *Junia: The First Woman Apostle*. He shows that (a) there are over 250 first-century inscriptions in Rome alone with the female name "Junia," (b) there is no evidence whatsoever in the Greek or Latin literature of the day for the existence of the male name "Junias," (c) there is no evidence whatsoever that the known male name "Junianus" was ever shortened to "Junias" or any other type of nickname, (d) the construction of the Greek wording in this verse should *not* be translated as "well known to the apostles," and (e) virtually all bible scholars and theologians up to about 1300 AD recognized that "Junia" was indeed a female name.

Consequently, after carefully exegeting the passage, Linda Belleville writes, "Thus the reading of this reference to Junia yields an example of a woman not only functioning as an 'apostle' in the New Testament church but being highly esteemed as such by Paul and his apostolic colleagues."[163]

Luke refers to the prophetic ministry of Philip's daughters (Acts 21:8-9). Paul and John also acknowledge the existence of female prophets in the early church.[164] Women prayed and prophesied in public (1 Corinthians 11:5). Paul suggests that a prophet, like an apostle, designated an official role (1 Corinthians 12:28-29).

Priscilla and her husband Aquila became significant leaders of the church in several different locations (Acts 18:18, 26; Romans 16:3; 1 Corinthians 16:19; 2 Timothy 4:19). In 1 Corinthians 16, Paul speaks of Aquila and Priscilla together having a congregation meeting in their house.

Priscilla is a good example of a woman teacher. Four times, Paul and Luke mention Priscilla before her husband, Aquila

---

163 Linda L. Bellevile, "Women Leaders in the Bible," in *Discovering Biblical Equality*, Ronald W. Pierce and Rebecca Merrill Goothuis, general eds. (Downers Grove, IL: InterVarsity, 2004), p. 120.
164 Patzia, p. 177.

(Acts 18:18, 26; Romans 16:3; 2 Timothy 4:19). Priscilla's role as teacher emerges when Apollos visited Ephesus. Scripture says, "When Priscilla and Aquila heard him [Apollos], they took him aside and explained the way of God to him more accurately" (Acts 18:24-26). The account shows her teaching role, and she is mentioned before her husband in connection with the instruction of Apollos. Apollos was "well-versed in the Scriptures" (18:24), and so the fact that they explained "the way of God to him more accurately" means they must have had sufficient expertise to gain his acceptance. Michael Green says,

> The New Testament tells us of women laboring in evangelism, acting as hostess to the church in their houses, prophesying and speaking in tongues, and acting as deaconesses. This prominence of women continued, as we have seen, in the second century. Sometimes it would be exercised through public speaking, sometimes through martyrdom.[165]

Some have used 1 Timothy 3:1 to prohibit women in ministry because some translations, like the NASB read, "It is a trustworthy statement: if any man aspires to the office of overseer, it is a fine work he desires to do." The problem in the Greek is that the word *man* in English does not appear in the Greek text. In the Greek, the word is *tis*, an indefinite pronoun. The masculine and feminine forms of this pronoun are identical, and indistinguishable as to gender apart from the context (The NIV translation is better, "If any one"). We've already seen that the early church was fluid and flowed naturally from the house church structure.

---

165 Green, Kindle edition, p. 247.

Although the New Testament does not directly designate a specific woman as an elder or bishop, we do find women acting in the kind of leadership functions normally associated with this office. Women exercised the authority of prophets, teachers, and apostolic coworkers. Stanley J. Grenz and Denise Muir Kjesbo write,

Paul readily spoke of women, as well as men, as his coworkers. He never cautioned his recipients to view only the men as possessing authority or being worthy of honor. Rather, his readers were to "submit to . . . everyone who joins in the work, and labors at it" (1 Corinthians 16:16).[166]

The New Testament paints a clear picture of women's role in ministry in the early church. It's beyond the scope of this book to provide an in-depth study of the three controversial passages about women in ministry: 1 Corinthians 11-14, 1 Timothy 2: 8-15, and 1 Timothy 3. However, I do write about these passages in detail elsewhere.[167]

LEADERSHIP ROLES

What about the office of bishop, pastor, and elder? In today's church these offices have become formalized and official. In the New Testament there was no bishop-pastor-elder hierarchy, in fact, they were interchangeable terms for the same role. A bishop/overseer" (Greek = *episkopos*) was also called a "pastor/shepherd" (Greek = *poimen*) and a "presbyter/elder" (Greek =

---

166 Grenz, Kjesbo, pp. 935-937.
167 I explain my convictions on these passages in detail here: http://www.joelcomiskey-group.com/articles/churchLeaders/women.htm

presbuteros), since all three terms in the Greek address the same group of people in Acts 20:17, 28 and 1 Pet 5:1-5.

Therefore, it seems that in the early church, those who assumed these titles were house church leaders or overseers of various house churches. Gehring, writing about these roles, says,

> Everything seems to indicate that they were overseers of the churches that met in their homes, much like Stephanas in Corinth; in other words, they were leaders of individual house churches. Together as a group such overseers could have formed the leadership team or council for the whole local church in that city.[168]

Arthur G. Patzia writes, "From the extant evidence it is possible to conclude that, at the time the Pastorals were written, bishops were overseers of local house churches and were assisted by a group of individuals identified as deacons."[169]

1 Timothy 3:1-3 and Titus 1:5-6 describe an overseer as a hospitable house leader with his domestic affairs in order. When Paul says that the overseer must have a good reputation with outsiders (1 Timothy 3:7), most likely he's envisioning a house church leader held in high esteem in the local society. If the leader had a bad reputation in the city, this would hinder the evangelistic outreach.[170] In the Pastoral Epistles, we see leaders who are supposed to exemplify a godly, well-ordered household to a pagan society (1 Timothy 2:4; 3:15; Titus 3:8).

---

168 Gehring, p. 206.
169 Patzia, p. 171.
170 Gehring, p. 265.

TEAMS OF LEADERS

The norm in the early church was to have a team of leaders over house churches. Paul, for example, told the leaders of the Ephesian church that the Holy Spirit had made them "overseers" of the flock (Acts 20:28). When writing to the church at Philippi, Paul greeted the congregation and, separately, the "overseers" (Philippians 1:1). When he wrote to Titus, Paul directed the appointment of elders, whom he also identified with the functions of "overseer" (Titus 1:5-7). Whether they are designated as a "body of elders" (1 Timothy 4:14) or simply as "elders," this form of leadership was always exercised by a group of people rather than by one single individual (Acts 20:17; 1 Timothy 5:17; Titus 1:5; James 5:14; 1 Peter 5:1-4). Michael Green says about early church leadership,

> Leadership was always plural: the word 'presbyter' from which we derive `priest' is regularly used in the plural when describing Christian ministry in the New Testament. They were a leadership team, supporting and encouraging one another, and doubtless making up for each other's deficiencies. This team leadership is very evident in the missionary journeys of the New Testament, and Acts 13:1 is particularly interesting. It indicates not only a plural leadership in Antioch, consisting of five members, but diverse types of leadership: some were 'prophets' relying on charismatic gifts, while others were 'teachers' relying on study of the Scriptures.[171]

Even the first apostles operated as a team. While guiding the Jerusalem church, they shared the leadership of the congregation

---

171 Green, Kindle edition p. 25.

with a group of elders (Acts 15:4, 6, 22), who remained long after the apostles were gone (Acts 21:18).

The New Testament writers avoid the idea of one, single leader. The norm for the early churches was to have a team of pastors rather than only one. In addition to overseers and/or elders, two churches are mentioned as having deacons (Philippians 1:1; 1 Timothy 3:8, 12). Whatever their functions may have been, their services were also provided on the basis of shared leadership since they are always mentioned in the plural.

The authors of *Home Cell Groups and House Churches* write, "There seems to have been a plurality of leaders in each congregation—certainly in each community of house churches in a given city. Moreover, these titles of leadership often seemed interchangeable with the same leaders being designated by more than one title."[172]

FLEXIBLE AND REPRODUCIBLE

We don't see a formal hierarchical structure in the New Testament like we see today. The gifts of the Spirit flowed among the house church members, and the gifted equippers developed the saints to continue the house-to-house growth.

Both men and women equally participated, and the New Testament writers used leadership titles sparingly. The elders and deacons emerged from the local house church structure.

Teams of leaders ministering together were simply the outgrowth of Christ's own ministry where he not only developed his own team, but also sent forth the disciples in pairs. And just as the leaders banded together, the house churches were not independent entities, but rather were connected to a larger network.

---

172 Hadaway, DuBose, Wright, p. 69.

Chapter Eight

ECCLESIAL NETWORKS:
HOW CHURCHES WERE
CONNECTED BEYOND THE HOME

In Bible college, my homiletics' professor instructed us to wind down our sermons after twenty-five minutes because most congregations couldn't handle more than a thirty minute message. I readily agreed because I wasn't sure if I could find enough material to go longer than thirty minutes.

Yet, as I look back, I don't remember talking about how long the apostles took in their sermons or whether or not they even stood behind a pulpit. And did they deliver sermons? I just assumed that a twenty-five minute sermon was biblical. I made similar assumptions about songs on Sunday, announcements, greetings, and church programs.

Perhaps I didn't ask enough questions. Maybe my professors didn't really know. Maybe it didn't matter because Sunday protocol was already well established in the Protestant church, and if it was good enough for other denominations, then we needed to follow.

As we go back to the primitive church and ask what they actually did in those celebration gatherings, we can only find principles and patterns, rather than dogmatic answers. We also need to be open to allow the New Testament to critique our own patterns today.

Finding clear answers about the celebration gatherings in the early church isn't so simple because of the relationships between individual house churches and city churches varied. We do find evidence, however, that house churches enjoyed relationship with one another and even met together periodically as a gathered church.

THE CONNECTION BETWEEN HOUSE CHURCHES

In Paul's letter to the Corinthians, he addresses the individual *ecclesia* that met in the home of Aquila and Priscilla (1 Corinthians 16:19), but he also greets the *ecclesia* as a whole (1 Corinthians 1:2 and 2 Corinthians 1:1). Wayne Meeks writes, "Paul imagined a connection between converts within a city, region, and province. . . . Paul wrote only one letter to a city or area, assuming it would suffice for all groups." [173]

The house churches that Paul planted, in other words, were part of a larger unit. Gehring writes, "Many NT scholars believe that both forms—small house churches and the whole church

---

173 As quoted in John L. White, *The Apostle of God* (Peabody, MA: Hendrickson, 1999), p. 207.

as a unit at that location—existed side by side in early Christianity."[174] Gehring goes on to say,

> The proof of a plurality of house churches alongside the whole church at one location would shed light on the controversial issue regarding the clarification of the relationship between the individual churches and the whole local church, and between the local church and the universal church.[175]

In other words, individual believers and house churches considered themselves part of a greater citywide church.

We also notice the existence of both public preaching as well as house-to-house ministry. For example, at times the whole church gathered in unidentified places for public ministry. In Acts 15:4, Luke writes, "When they came to Jerusalem, they were welcomed by the church and the apostles and elders, to whom they reported everything God had done through them."

Later on in Acts 15:22 we read, "Then the apostles and elders, with the whole church, decided to choose some of their own men and send them to Antioch with Paul and Barnabas." The individual house churches were linked by leadership that occasionally gathered the house churches together.

Paul's own leadership, for example, was crucial in linking house churches together. We see Paul and Silas in Acts 16:4 traveling from town to town, delivering the decisions reached by the apostles and elders in Jerusalem. We're not sure exactly where they had those discussions, but we do see the leadership connection within the house church network. Ken Giles, writing about this leadership link, says,

---

174 Gehring, p. 25.
175 Gehring, p. 26.

It is often assumed that in the New Testament age there were no institutional structures linking individual congregations or local churches to the wider Christian community, but this is not true. The institutional forms that were needed and were appropriate for this period began to appear very early. In the Book of Acts, Luke maintains that a group of elders with general oversight of the Christian community in Jerusalem was in place by the time the church at Antioch was established.[176]

I've mentioned the Acts 15 passage earlier as an example of this leadership link, but Paul says something similar in 1 Timothy 4:14, "Do not neglect your gift, which was given you through a prophetic message when the body of elders laid their hands on you."

In the Jerusalem church, those leadership associations were especially clear because we read, "Day after day, in the temple courts and from house to house, they never stopped teaching and proclaiming the good news that Jesus is the Christ" (Acts 5:42). In the Jerusalem church, the apostolic leadership gathered together the various house churches.

These gatherings of the whole church can also be seen in Acts 21:5. Paul is making his way back to the Jerusalem church after his mission trip to the Gentiles, and the Scripture says, "But when our time was up, we left and continued on our way. All the disciples and their wives and children accompanied us out of the city, and there on the beach we knelt to pray."

Because the early church had no permanent buildings or specific meeting places, they used a variety of meeting places for the larger gatherings, and on this particular occasion, they gathered on the beach. We don't have specific knowledge of all

---

176 Giles, 1995, p. 188.

the early public places, but we do know that public gatherings existed (Acts 20:20).

Throughout this book, we've learned that the primary meeting venue was the house. The public gatherings, therefore, seem to be the gathering of the various house churches together in whatever meeting places were available. We do know of a few of these public places.

Paul used the lecture hall of Tyrannus in Corinth where Scripture says, "He took the disciples with him and had discussions daily" (Acts 19:9). At times the whole church met in larger homes, like in the case of the upper room where the disciples met in preparation for the Spirit's descent (Acts 1:12; 2:1).

In Rome, Paul sends greetings from the "whole church" who he had gathered together. Romans 16:23 says, "Gaius, whose hospitality I and the whole church here enjoy, sends you his greetings." Paul refers here to the whole church meeting together in one large home, but the point is that the various house churches did come together to celebrate.[177]

GATHERED HOUSE CHURCHES IN A LARGER MEETING

We don't have a lot of information about the larger celebration gatherings in all parts of the Mediterranean region. However, we do know that the individual house churches celebrated together in Jerusalem and Corinth.

In Jerusalem, the early church met in houses to participate in the Lord's Supper and fellowship, but then those same house churches gathered together in the temple to hear the apostles teaching. Acts 2:46-47 says, "Every day they continued to meet

---

177 Robert and Julia Banks, 1986, p. 40.

together in the temple courts. They broke bread in their homes and ate together with glad and sincere hearts, praising God and enjoying the favor of all the people. And the Lord added to their number daily those who were being saved." We see here both the house church meetings as well as those house churches coming together to hear the apostles teaching. Gehring writes,

> It can be inferred from our text that the primitive church gathered for two different types of worship services, which can be distinguished from one another on the basis not only of their locality but of their organizational arrangement as well. The main emphasis in the house was on bread breaking. The first Christians likely took part in the temple prayers held in the temple courts, and from there they went into the hall of Solomon for a gathering of the whole congregation, with the emphasis on missionary proclamation and biblical instruction.[178]

The community life of the Jerusalem church was enhanced by both the small group as well as the large group experience. They enjoyed the intimate community of the Lord's Supper in homes, but received solid teaching in the larger gathering. Writing about the Jerusalem church, Gerhard Lohfink says,

> The believers are a single assembly even though the place of their assembly changes. They meet in the Temple to praise God publicly. This shows their claim to be the eschatological Israel. But they also met in private houses to celebrate the Lord's supper. Again the unanimity of their assembly is emphasized. [179]

---

178 Gehring, pp. 81-82.
179 Lohfink, p. 224.

David Shenk and Irvin Stutzman break down the early church activity further,

> The first congregations were house churches which met in small clusters throughout the Jerusalem metropolitan area. Since most of the homes in the Jerusalem area were small, we may assume that from ten to twenty people gathered in each of these cell group fellowships. Probably 100-200 of these small congregations, meeting in living rooms throughout the Jerusalem area, were formed within days of Pentecost. Yet they never functioned independently of each other. These home cell groups formed the clusters comprising the church in Jerusalem, a congregation who for some time met around the temple area for celebration events.[180]

As we've already seen, the house sizes differed, and we really don't know how many house churches existed in the Jerusalem area. We only know that they came together under the leadership of the apostles to hear the apostles' teaching and to celebrate the resurrected Christ, just like Acts 5:42 says.

Similarly, in Acts 5:12, we notice that, "The apostles performed many miraculous signs and wonders among the people. And all the believers used to meet together in Solomon's Colonnade." Solomon's Colonnade was basically a publicly accessible porch or veranda outside the East Gate of Jerusalem's Temple site that could accommodate a huge group of people.

The second clear example is in Corinth. Paul says, " So if the whole church comes together and everyone speaks in tongues, and some who do not understand or some unbelievers come

---

180 David W. Shenk and Ervin R. Stutzman, *Creating Communities of the Kingdom: New Testament Models of Church Planting* (Scottdale, PA: Herald Press, 1988), p. 92.

in, will they not say that you are out of your mind?" (1 Corinthians 14:23). Paul speaking about the whole church coming together implies that at other times the Christians in Corinth met separately in smaller house churches. Yet, both were considered the *church*. Arthur G. Patzia writes,

> All this illustrates that "the church of God that is in Corinth" (1 Corinthians 1:2) and the "whole church" (holes tes ekklesias) mentioned in Romans 16:23 consisted of several local house churches, each one somewhat different in its ethnic, social and economic mix of people. Paul's reference to "the church of God in Corinth" (1 Corinthians 1:2) and to the believers coming together "as a church" (1 Corinthians 11:18), along with the implication that Gaius was hosting the entire (holes) church (Romans 16:23), suggest that there were occasions in Corinth when all the believers assembled. In time, these letters were shared with other churches in the city and read at their worship services before a redactor collected and edited them into their current format as 1 and 2 Corinthians.[181]

Gehring envisions the small groups meeting separately to focus on the Lord's Supper and then at other times assembling together to hear the preaching of the word, much like what happened in the Jerusalem church.[182] In his book, *The Theology of Paul the Apostle*, James Dunn notes the large church/small church emphasis in Corinth when he writes,

> Paul could speak both of the whole congregation in a place as "church" and also of individual house groups within that congregation as "church" (1 Cor. 1:1; 16:19). The one was

---

181 Patzia, p. 192.
182 Gehring, p. 172.

not seen as detracting from the status of the other. Wherever believers met together, they were "the church of God." The implication of 1 Cor. 16:19 set alongside 14:23 (referring to the whole church meeting together) is probably that church gatherings consisted of more regular small house groups interspersed with less frequent (weekly, monthly?) gatherings of the "the whole church." [183]

Dunn speculates about more regular house church meetings interspersed with less frequent celebration gatherings. This seems like a logical conclusion because the smaller house meetings would have been more feasible and practical. Gathering in larger groups in public places would have been more difficult logistically—and at times dangerous.

Even though the early church in Jerusalem *met daily* in public gatherings, at least for awhile, it's unlikely that this practice continued. All we can say with accuracy is that the small and large group format existed both in Jerusalem and Corinth.[184]

What about the house churches in other parts of the Mediterranean world? How often did they meet in house meetings and combined gatherings? We've already seen Paul's greeting to the whole church in Rome. Most likely Paul gathered the entire church in a larger house church setting periodically because in Romans 16:23 he uses the same terminology he used

---

183 James D.G. Dunn, *The Theology of Paul the Apostle* (Grand Rapids, MI: Eerdmans, 1998), p. 541.

184 Rad Zdero writes, "The church in Jerusalem made use of it [the temple] for large group events as a supplement to home group meetings. First, believers frequented the Temple courts, possibly en masse, often for evangelism, healing events, teaching, and/or prayer. Second, large group gatherings also happened when there was a controversial topic that needed to be discussed. For example, believers met over the controversial topic of what to do with non-Jews who were becoming Christians (Rad Zdero, "Apostolic Strategies for Growing and Connecting the Early House Churches," in *Nexus: The World House Church Movement Reader*, Pasadena CA: William Carey Library, 2007, p. 127)

in Corinth, "Gaius, whose hospitality I and the whole church here enjoy, sends you his greetings."

In Ephesus, we see Paul's pattern of teaching publically and from house-to-house (Acts 20:20). The larger group gathering can also be seen in Paul's greeting from all the churches in Asia (1 Corinthians 16:19). As part of Paul's general greeting to the churches in Asia, he then specifically mentions the house church of Aquila and Priscilla and their particular greetings to the churches. Paul seems to imply that there were other Christians in Ephesus who did not meet at Aquila's home. This, along with the relatively large size of the church in Ephesus, suggests a plurality of house churches there.[185]

F.F. Bruce comments, "Such house churches appear to have been smaller circles of fellowship within the larger fellowship of the city *ecclesia*."[186] Paul would gather this larger *ecclesia* to preach and teach publicly but would also minister from house-to-house.

The same can be said about the church in Thessalonica. Paul writes to the entire church in his introduction, "To the church of the Thessalonians in God the Father and the Lord Jesus Christ" (1:1). Like in the case of the church in Rome and Ephesus, we can assume that the church in Thessalonica was broken down into house churches. Most likely the house groups gathered for special celebration events, as when Paul sailed from Philippi after the Feast of Unleavened Bread, and joined other believers at Troas (Acts 20:6).

If there were five hundred thousand believers by the end of the first century as Robert T. Glover suggests, there must have been countless house churches. Most likely those house

---

185 Gehring, p. 144.
186 Frederick F. Bruce, *The Epistles to the Ephesians and Colossians* (Grand Rapids, MI: Eerdmans, 1957), p. 310.

churches gathered for occasional worship as we saw in the Jerusalem and Corinth examples.

PAUL'S DIFFERENT USAGES OF "CHURCH"

Even though Christians in the New Testament used *ecclesia* to refer to the church, the normal secular use of the word simply referred to a gathering of people. For example, the word *ecclesia* is used of a secular gathering in Acts 19:21-41 when the silversmiths gathered together to conspire against Paul and the preaching of the gospel, "The assembly [*ecclesia*] was in confusion: Some were shouting one thing, some another. Most of the people did not even know why they were there."

Whenever a gathering or assembly took place in the Greek culture, it was called *ecclesia*. Christians, of course, gave that gathering special significance, but the root meaning is simply a "gathered group of people."[187] The early church used it to refer to those united together by their common bond with Christ. The word became an affirmation of the church's special corporate identity. Gerhard Lohfink gives added insight, "The real origin of *ecclesia* of God is the Old Testament and the Jewish traditions of speech that derived from it. Ultimately *ecclesia* points to the people of God gathered at Sinai."[188]

The New Testament writers use *ecclesia* to refer to the church in a local area or in a broader geographical area. Both the local, singular form (Acts 11:26; 13:1; 14:27; 15:3; 18:22; 20:17) and plural form of the word (Acts 15:41; 16:5) are used for the church.

In other words, *ecclesia* encompassed all believers living in a large city (Acts 11:22; 13:1; 1 Corinthians 1:2) as well as the

---

187 Banks, 1995, p. 27
188 Lohfink, p. 219.

ecclesia in the home. Alan Richardson writes, "The technical meaning of *ecclesia* can be summed up without reference to size, location, or official organization: "*ecclesia* calls us to see believers-in-community."[189]

Let's look at the three uses of the term a little deeper.

All Christians on Earth

Paul uses *ecclesia* to refer to all believers, or the universal church. This is implied when Paul says, "Do not cause anyone to stumble, whether Jews, Greeks or the church of God" (1 Corinthians 10:32). The same can be said of 1 Corinthians 12:28 where Paul addresses the entire church, "And in the church [*ecclesia*] God has appointed first of all apostles, second prophets, third teachers, then workers of miracles, also those having gifts of healing, those able to help others, those with gifts of administration, and those speaking in different kinds of tongues."

All Christians In One Location

At times Paul addresses the entire church in the city (1 Thessalonians 1:1; 2 Thessalonians 1:1; 1 Corinthians 1:2; 2 Corinthians 1:1 and Romans 16:1). In other places, Paul uses *ecclesia* to refer to a larger geographical district, such as Asia or Galatia (1 Corinthians 16:1, 19). For example, "the churches in the province of Asia" (1 Corinthians 16:19) is a broad statement about believers in a major district. The "Macedonian churches"

---

189 Alan Richardson, s.v. "Church," in *A Theological Word Book of the Bible* (New York: The Macmillan Company, 1960), p. 48; K. L. Schmidt, op. cit., p. 506.

(2 Corinthians 8:1) were the Christian communities within the region of Macedonia.

When Paul uses the expression *church of God* he usually has in mind the gathering of Christians who lived at a specific location. In 1 Corinthians 1:1-2 Paul speaks to the Corinthian church as the "church of God in Corinth."

A Small Christian Group Who Regularly Met In a Home

Paul also used the word *ecclesia* to refer to the church in private homes. We've repeatedly mentioned examples of this throughout the book in places like:

- Romans 16:3-5: Greet Priscilla and Aquila. . . . Greet also the church that meets at their house.
- Philemon 2: Apphia our sister, to Archippus our fellow soldier and to the church that meets in your home.

This is the sense that Paul uses most of the time when using the word *ecclesia*.[190] Paul does not indicate that there is any fundamental difference between the smallest house church and the whole church of God. God is equally present in his fullness in both scenarios.[191] Bill Beckham writes, "To be consistent with New Testament usage, *ecclesia* cannot be called church in one place (the large group expression) and not called church in another (the small group expression)."[192]

---

190 Millard Erickson, *Christian Theology* (Grand Rapids, MI: Baker Book House, 1998), p. 1043.
191 Gehring, p. 165.
192 Bill Beckham, "Confirming Governing Principles That Will Guide the Second Stage of the Cell Church Network in Brazil," doctoral degree prospectus (San Francisco, CA: Golden Gate Baptist Seminary, 2011), p. 22.

Some today look at the Sunday celebration as the true church, but small groups as less than the real church. Others tend to prioritize house churches as opposed to the gathered church. From this brief review of Paul's use of the word *ecclesia*, we see both views of the church as being important and even vital.

PUBLICLY AND FROM HOUSE-TO-HOUSE

In the New Testament, the house church setting was the main focus of growth and discipleship for the early believers. Yet, God blessed the gathering of those house churches together to make them more effective. He developed gifted leaders to serve the individual house churches and to instruct them publically.

At certain time periods, the house churches gathered frequently into a larger celebration service. Yet it appears that most of the time the house churches only occasionally met together for combined worship and teaching. Whether gathered or scattered, the primitive churches were not separate, independent entities. They were connected to a greater apostolic leadership vision. Each type of gathering was fully considered the ecclesia.

Part 3

ECCLESIAL LIFE
TODAY

Chapter Nine

CELL CHURCH ECCLESIOLOGY TODAY

In 2001, my family and I moved back to the United States after eleven years of serving as missionaries in Ecuador. While working as a missionary pastor in churches in Quito, I experienced cell group growth that could only be described as explosive church growth. I spent a lot of time and energy analyzing the core principles of that growth, so I could help others replicate that growth.

When we started our church in Southern California, I assumed I would be able to import those principles and experience the same explosive growth. However, that was not the case. The problem was not with the principles, but with how those principles played out in different cultures. Southern

California is vastly different than Ecuador, to say the least. I had to rethink the principles and work through what they meant in the culture where I now live.

As I have gone through the process of writing this book, I have been reminded about my cultural transition from Ecuador to Southern California. In some ways, entering into the world of the first century was a similar, surprising experience as was adjusting to life in Ecuador. I have discovered many things that I did not expect to find.

So what do we do with the historical evidence analyzed in the previous chapters?

This question is especially important because the Western world is so different than the world of the first century church. They typically lived in small houses that were built adjacent to one another. Many today live in private homes with walled security fences. Their lifestyle centered on the home, which included working, eating, and playing. We drive to work. We drive to go out to eat. And we drive to our play. Their time of relaxation was full of food, conversation, and time with family and neighbors. Our time of relaxation is focused on television, the internet, and video games.

So how do we implement what we have learned about life in the New Testament church? How does it apply to us who live in twenty-first century Southern California, or Rockport, Maine, or Heidelberg, Germany, or Toronto, Canada, or Hong Kong, or Sao Paulo, Brazil? What does it have to do with us, who live and work right here, right now?

BIBLICAL THEOLOGY AS THE FOUNDATION FOR CELL GROUPS

Chapter 1 Review:

Theology breeds methodology. A theological foundation for doing cell ministry will sustain the pastor or church over time. Unstable foundations include church growth, church health, spiritual revelation, or following the latest fad. Pseudo foundations include superficial proof texting of Scripture or reading into the Bible personal prejudices or presuppositions. A true biblical theology requires understanding the biblical context and worldview of Scripture before applying it to today.

How solid is the foundation for your cell group strategy? With this question, I encourage you to go beyond mere thoughts about what you should call your groups. You might not like the term cells or cell church. Or you might see yourself as a committed cell church pastor or leader, but that does not mean your foundation is strong. I also encourage you to look deeper than the author or church model that has influenced you the most. This is not a question about with whom you line up or about those with whom you disagree.

A foundation that will carry you through the ups and downs of cell groups is not based on a theology that you have. It's based on a theology that has you. If you are doing cell groups because they work, or because your people need community, or because they can close the back door, your foundation will crumble when groups aren't working well, when conflict arises, or when people become too busy to participate.

Even cognitive reasons based on the biblical evidence compiled in this book must go beyond mental ascent to the point that they become some of the core convictions of your heart, soul, and mind. That's the kind of foundational vision that grabs you and won't let go. You become "compelled" as the Apostle Paul wrote in 1 Corinthians 9:16.

It's what you must do, not because it works, although groups do work rather nicely. Not because it will make your church successful, although groups can make your church more successful. Not because you have to be the right kind of church, although groups can help you become the right kind of church. You follow this path because the vision for doing life together, mutual accountability, hospitality, deeper discipleship, organic church life in our neighborhoods, and the call to take the gospel into everyday life has shaken your soul and moved you from the inside out. You can do nothing else.

The research and insights found in this book are meant to provide a compelling cognitive foundation for you to develop your core convictions that will build your cell groups on a strong foundation. However, you cannot copy these convictions from this book or any other. You have to articulate the key convictions that you and your church will use as the foundation for cell groups.

At a church-wide level, these convictions will provide the core elements of the teaching and training that will establish the cell ministry in your church. Convictions about the themes of family, community, relational outreach, hospitality, and simple leadership development must be articulated and become a normal part of the language of your church.

One way to do this is to summarize the main points of each chapter in your own language and share those principles with your elders, cell leaders, and cell members. Work through the challenges of making these themes a regular part of church life.

The way we use words is important, and if we fail to develop a language that matches the strategy and structure of our cell groups, we will remain stuck with a language that fits our programmatic, non-relational ways of doing church.

At the cell group level, these convictions will challenge group members to actually live out the call to be a family. They will help members understand why the cell groups meet every week, even though busy modern life fights against it. It teaches them about working through conflict when the cultural pattern is to run from it. And it calls everyone to minister and offer their gifts to the community and to their lost friends and family, even though we have assumed that only those with spiritual positions can really minister as God intended.

Take some time to examine your own values about cell groups. What have you written regarding the reasoning behind cell group ministry? What is listed on your website? What are the reasons provided in your training? How do your sermons reflect those values? Look at your core convictions about groups. Name them. Think through the unstated core values about groups, elders, staff, and key volunteers.

Some questions to ask:

1. Are you basing church ministry on biblical theology or pragmatic reasoning?
2. Are your motivations based on God's Word?
3. Are you pressing ahead in cell ministry because you understand that biblical discipleship demands it?
4. Are you energized by the biblical basis for cell ministry?

CHURCH THAT REFLECTS THE CHARACTER OF
GOD

Chapter 2 Review:
There is one God who exists in three persons: Father, Son, and Holy Spirit. God lives in community and desires that human beings also live in love and unity. God created humankind in his image and his imagine is inherently relational. Isolationism goes against God's nature, and God calls his church to reflect community. The good news is that God is working within believers to make them more relational.

What way of life is viewed by most people as embodying personal success? Money? Check! Freedom? Check! Autonomy? Check! In my ministry, I've traveled around the globe training churches. I have found that many people share a common assumption that those in the West, specifically the United States, live very successful lives.

Alexis de Tocqueville, a French sociologist from the nineteenth century, studied the way Americans live and attributed their success to "individualism." He wrote, "Individualism is a calculated and considered feeling which disposes each citizen to isolate himself from the mass of his fellows and withdraw into the circle of family and friends."[193] He also observed,

---

193 Quoted in Robert N. Bellah, et. al., *Habits of the Heart* (Berkley: University of California Press, 1996), p. 37.

As democratic individualism grows, there are more and more people who, though neither rich nor powerful enough to have much hold over others, have gained or kept enough wealth and enough understanding to look after their own needs. Such folk owe no man anything and hardly expect anything from anybody. They form the habit of thinking of themselves in isolation and imagine that they hold destiny in their hands.[194]

Since Tocqueville's research, many cultural observers and sociologists have stated these conclusions in their own ways. The malaise of individualism is the air we breathe and because there is a hunger for success, more and more people buy into individualism as a way of everyday life.

Sadly, the church has often failed to call this life pattern into question. In fact, the primary motivation in many Protestant circles is to reinforce it. Personal salvation, personal discipleship, and one's personal destiny were at the heart of so many sermons I grew up hearing almost every week. We assumed that the individual's relationship to God was primary and that involvement in the church had the purpose of reinforcing that personal relationship.

Christian literature often promotes this subtle form of individualism. Once I asked a group of pastors I was coaching to read *Revolution* by George Barna. Yet, I failed to read it thoroughly before giving it to the pastors. Later, after carefully reading it, I realized Barna was encouraging believers to form their own "individualized church." Barna writes about believers choosing from a proliferation of options that constitutes the

---

194 Bellah, p. 37.

"personal church" of the individual.[195]   When we met as a coaching group several weeks later to study the book, I had to apologize for my hasty promotion of the book and then pinpointed out its weak theology.

This individualistic way of thinking has infiltrated the way we do cell groups more than we realize. Because we enter into group life with an individualist mindset, people participate in groups as long as they receive something beneficial. They assume that their personal growth is the top priority and fail to see how God is creating a people that reflect his character together. Then when troubles come along or the group proves less than beneficial, they move on to something else, not even realizing that an individualist consumer mentality drives them away from God's plan for community life.

The church is called to reflect God's relational, triune character. The cell group is much more than a weekly meeting designed to meet an individual's need for a personal church. It's a manifestation of God's life now, today--or at least there's the potential for that. It's a chance for face-to-face interaction that will bring us in contact with people and a chance to practice community. Learning to submit to one another and practicing humble service to brothers and sisters pleases God because this is how the three persons of the Trinity relate to one another.

God's character is revealed through leaders who are in team ministry, are learning to serve in love and unity. It confronts and expels the dictator mentality, expressed in some cell church leadership models, where one person leads through fear and control.

---

195 George Barna, *Revolution* (Wheaton, Illinois: Tyndale House, 2005). I have a complete review of this book at http://www.joelcomiskeygroup.com/articles/bookRe-views/BarnaRevolution.htm. Barna talks about replacing the local church with various "micro-model" options which might be: a worship conference, coaching communities, internet groups, parachurch ministries (p. 66). And this is probably Barna's crown jewel phrase: "personalized church."

This is why the *one anothers* of the New Testament are so vital to the life of the church.[196] They directly confront the individualism of our culture and help us reflect the character of God. We need each other. The term in the Bible for *one another* is a reciprocal pronoun meaning "mutual ministry." I've created categories that make the biblically based *one anothers* more easily understood. These broad categories are:

- Focusing on others
- Accountability
- Interdependence
- Watchfulness

Focusing on Others

We naturally focus on our own needs and wants. Someone said that when you're fifteen years old, you are concerned about what others think about you. When you're forty-five, you really don't care what people think about you. When you're sixty-five, you realize that no one was thinking about you anyway!

The truth is that we spend most of our time thinking about ourselves. The triune God longs to guide us to focus on others. Some of the *one anothers* that fit under this category include:

Love One Another
"A new command I give you: Love one another. As I have loved you, so you must love one another. By this all men will know that you are my disciples, if you love one another" (John 13:34-35).

---

196 I go into much more detail on the topic of the *one anothers* of Scripture in my book, *Relational Disciple* (Moreno Valley, CA: CCS Publishing, 2009).

Serve One Another
"Not so with you. Instead, whoever wants to become great among you must be your servant, and whoever wants to be first must be slave of all. For even the Son of Man did not come to be served, but to serve, and to give his life as a ransom for many" (Mark 10:43-45).

Forgive Each Other
"Forgive as the Lord forgave you" (Colossians 3:13).

Build Up Each Other
"So then let us pursue the things which make for peace and the building up of one another" (Romans 14:19, NASV).

Encourage Each Other
"Therefore encourage one another and build each other up, just as in fact you are doing" (1 Thessalonians 5:11).

Be Kind to One Another
"Be kind and compassionate to one another" (Ephesians 4:32).

Be Devoted to One Another
"Be devoted to one another in brotherly love" (Romans 12:10). The word *devoted* might be translated "kindly affectionate." Paul had the devotion of a family in mind.

Accountability

None of us are lone rangers on this journey in Christ's kingdom. Rather, we are fellow travelers on the same heavenly bound journey. Scripture tells us to look out for one another and hold each other accountable. The early church held each other accountable, and we need to do the same today.

Instruct One Another

"Let the word of Christ richly dwell within you, with all wisdom teaching and admonishing one another with psalms and hymns and spiritual songs, singing with thankfulness in your hearts to God" (Colossians 3:16, NASV).

Submit to One Another

"Submit to one another out of reverence for Christ" (Ephesians 5:21).

Confess Sins to One Another

"Therefore confess your sins to each other and pray for each other so that you may be healed. The prayer of a righteous man is powerful and effective" (James 5:16).

Interdependence

Our sinful nature tends to exalt self before others. Scripture tells us we need to look upon our brothers and sisters as more important than ourselves. This is a supernatural activity because we are naturally born selfish. Paul says,

> I hope in the Lord Jesus to send Timothy to you soon, that I also may be cheered when I receive news about you. I have no one else like him, who takes a genuine interest in your welfare. For everyone looks out for his own interests, not those of Jesus Christ (Philippians 2:19-21).

It requires a supernatural work of grace to go beyond our own selfishness and think about the needs of others. It's hard to get beyond our own egos and actually think about what others are experiencing and what they are going through. Yet, this is love.

Walk In Humility with One Another
"Clothe yourselves with humility toward one another, for God is opposed to the proud but gives grace to the humble" (1 Peter 5:5, NASV).

Accept One Another
"Accept one another, then, just as Christ accepted you, in order to bring praise to God" (Romans 15:7).

Live at Peace with One Another
"Live in peace with one another" (1 Thessalonians 5:13b).

Bear with Each Other
"Carry each other's burdens, and in this way you will fulfill the law of Christ" (Galatians 6:2).

Wait for One Another
"So then, my brothers, when you come together to eat, wait for each other. If anyone is hungry, he should eat at home, so that when you meet together it may not result in judgment" (1 Corinthians 11:33-34).

Honor One Another
"Honor one another above yourselves" (Romans 12:10).

Use Your Gifts among Each Other
"Each one should use whatever gift he has received to serve others, faithfully administering God's grace in its various forms. If anyone speaks, he should do it as one speaking the very words of God. If anyone serves, he should do it with the strength God provides, so that in all things God may be praised through Jesus Christ. To him be the glory and the power for ever and ever. Amen" (1 Peter 4:10-11).

Show Hospitality to One Another
Offer hospitality to one another without grumbling" (1 Peter 4:9).

Watchfulness

Most of the *one another* verses are positive. Yet, Scripture also warns believers against the invasion of the sinful nature. And this nature, like the devil himself, is prone to kill, steal, and destroy (John 10: 10). God calls relational disciples to reflect his character, and to avoid the opposite tendencies.

Do Not Lie to Each Other
"Do not lie to each other, since you have taken off your old self with its practices" (Colossians 3:9).

Do Not Fight with Each Other
"And the Lord's servant must not quarrel; instead, he must be kind to everyone, able to teach, not be resentful. Those who oppose him he must gently instruct, in the hope that God will grant them repentance leading them to a knowledge of the truth, and that they will come to their senses and escape from the trap of the devil, who has taken them captive to do his will" (2 Timothy 2:24-26).

Do Not Envy One Another
 "Let us not become conceited, provoking and envying each other" (Galatians 5:26).

Do Not Judge One Another
"Therefore let us stop passing judgment on one another. Instead, make up your mind not to put any stumbling block or obstacle in your brother's way" (Romans 14:13).

Although we live in this world, we are part of another one. The new world order is radically different than this one, and it follows the patterns of servanthood and love for one another. The good news is that God desires to conform us to his Trinitarian nature to fulfill the one another passages of Scripture.

Some questions to ask:

1. When was the last time you reflected on the Trinity? When was the last time you preached on God's triune nature?
2. Does God's triune nature guide the way you do ministry?
3. Is your church growing in unity?
4. Are the members of your cell group working through conflicts and growing in love for one another?
5. Does love characterize all you do as a church?

CHURCH AS FAMILY: IS IT POSSIBLE TODAY?

Chapter 3 Review:

God created families to reflect his triune nature. The first families from Genesis onward, grew, expanded, and filled the earth. However, the nation of Israel often failed to demonstrate God's character, and God sent his son, Jesus, to establish a new family, the church. The image of family is the primary metaphor for life in the New Testament church. God forged the church, his new family, in houses to reflect a close-knit, one another relationship, where hospitality and the extended family was the priority.

When we preach about things like God as our Father, other Christians as brothers and sisters, and the church as the family of God, there are at least two challenges to our modern situation.

First, for many in our churches, any reference to a familial image raises negative experiences. The high rate of divorce, the proliferation of abuse within family systems, and the absenteeism that defines much modern-day parenting sets a stage for many in our churches to resist any kind of familial experience. They do not want to repeat an experience of abandonment, misunderstanding, and pain from their past.

It's easier for people to embrace something like a modern business model for cell groups. People can envision the church like a business and pastors like CEOs who are hired to create church goods and services. The cell group is one those goods. Dr. Les Brickman writes,

> It is my observation that many cell churches, regardless of the motif presented, create cells out of a business or sports paradigm, rather than out of a family paradigm. From the beginning, it has been God's intention that His people exist as a community. This reflects the very nature of the triune God as Father, Son and Holy Spirit. God, though one, is an expression of community. Our lives are lived out in community as families, tribes and nations. Only within the context of a living dynamic community can we understand our responsibility and accountability to one another. The church as community originated in the mind of God. His activity brought it into being. He has given it its structure, its ministry as well as its mission.[197]

---

197 Les Brickman, *Preparing the 21st Century Church* (Fairfax, VA: Xulon Press, 2002), p. 133.

Familial imagery describes what it means to be the people of God. We cannot avoid this. It is the ruling metaphor that we cannot displace. We cannot adopt a way of doing church and groups that works better because it accommodates modern sensibilities.

When we adopt a business model, attendees hop from church to church because they see the church as a business, and they figure they should get the best "deal" by looking for the best worship service in town. Even within one local church, they hop from cell group to cell group because they are looking for what serves them best.

This leads us to the second modern-day challenge to viewing the church as family. When we think about a healthy family experience in the modern setting, it is vastly different from that found in the first century culture. In fact, the modern Western nuclear family, comprised of a unit of parents and children who operate independently of an extended family, is unique when compared to almost every culture in the history of humanity.

The image of family in the New Testament connotes an extended family with a patriarch or household leader of some kind, aunts and uncles, parents, and children, and also hired servants, indentured servants and their immediate families. Of course, I'm generalizing here. The families of the first century churches were more complex than this description, and they were not perfect by any means. For people in contemporary churches to experience church as family, there are a few things that can help point us in the right direction.

Teach Church as Family

Promoting the family nature of the church to the congregation will help people understand why they congregate and how the church should function. The family imagery will also critique the idea of individual salvation that is separated from the church. Hellerman writes,

> In the New Testament era a person was not saved for the sole purpose of enjoying a personal relationship with God. Indeed, the phrase "personal relationship with God" is found nowhere in the Bible. According to the New Testament, a person is saved to community. Salvation included membership in God's group. We are saved "into one body," . . . when we get a new Father we also get a new set of brothers and sisters. In Scripture salvation is a community-creating event.[198]

While we need to teach that each person receives Christ's salvation individually, we must not promote salvation apart from sanctification, and sanctification takes place in the family of God, Christ's church.

On a cell level, teach the home group members to be transparent—being willing to go to each other, rather than gossiping. Teach them to welcome those who are different—racially, economically, socially, and at different levels spiritually. Families welcome diversity.

We must teach our people about the implications of church as family, which is a core stream that runs through all of the theology I've developed in this book.

---

198 Hellerman, p. 124.

Experience Church as Family

Most people need to experience church as family before they will understand what the Bible teaches about it. Family is a lived truth, not an abstract one. Teaching sets the stage, but the real learning happens in the cell groups.

If your groups are especially weak in this area, brainstorm ways with other leaders about how to develop this experience organically. It cannot be instituted from the top down. Identify a few groups that either already experience true family life or experience aspects of family life. Invite them to come together and talk about what they are doing. Develop a list of ideas of how the family experience could be expanded. Ask them to be honest about what the church needs to change to reflect the biblical image of family.

For new believers and new members who come to your church through the large group worship, have them experience the family dynamic as soon as possible. Connect them to groups that experience church as family. Explain to them that this is the point of our life together. If that's not what they want, then at least they know your church's core philosophy.

Finally, one of the most important parts of the experience of family is the way children are included in the vision for groups. In many cases, we want groups that do not include children. In fact, we don't even see them as a part of the cell group vision. They are a part of the children's ministry. Yet, church as family means including multi-generational groups. No one has taught this more effectively than Daphne Kirk.[199]

---

199 Daphne Kirk is an international teacher and author on inter-generational cell groups. Two of her most popular books are: "Reconnecting the Generations" and "Born for Such a Time as This." Both books can be purchased at http://www.gnation2gnation.com

Appoint someone in your leadership to address the question of including children in group life. Children should be a part of the conversation when it comes to group strategies and group leadership meetings. At the very least, allow children to experience cell life by inviting them to participate in certain parts of the cell meeting. Then provide children with a separate teaching that specifically addresses their needs.

Share Church as Family

Church as a family also means we welcome those who are lonely and isolated and do not have a family. The new family that Jesus came to establish was not based on blood relationships, but on a new spiritual reality. Jesus welcomed all people to join that new family. We must do the same.

One of the main reasons the early church grew so rapidly was because it welcomed newcomers into the extended family, and then continued the process of multiplication to make sure there was room for everyone in God's family. House church extension was the natural step to reach more people for Jesus.

We must encourage church members to reach out to people who desperately need community and a place to belong. You can do this through special outreach events in both cell and celebration.

Leaders must model what they are asking others to do by participating in cell ministry and relational evangelism. One practical way to do this is to ask key leaders to model family life, either by leading a cell group or participating in one. This will strengthen your family emphasis when the church sees the leaders practicing what they're preaching.

Some questions to ask:

1. Is your church acting like a family? What are some of the ways you can improve in this area?
2. Is your church connecting with those who don't know Jesus through a web of family relationships?
3. Do cell members reach out to new people, inviting them into their cell family?
4. Do you welcome people in both cell and celebration to join God's family?
5. Are you ministering to children in the cell and celebration?
6. Are your key leaders leading a cell group or participating in one?

CHRIST'S MINISTRY AND TODAY'S CHURCH

Chapter 4 Review:

Jesus Christ came to proclaim God's rule, his kingdom. Christ gathered a community of disciples to demonstrate how this new kingdom operated. He chose ministry in homes to reflect the image of the new family of God. He then sent his disciples in teams to minister in houses, giving them clear instructions on how to reach people through the house strategy.

What would Jesus do? This was the question raised by Charles Sheldon in his famous book, *In His Steps*. What would Jesus do today, if he were living in your neighborhood? In your city? Attending your church?

Let's think about this in a different way. How would Jesus lead if he were guiding your church? Would he preach? How would he preach? Would he have a staff? How would he lead his staff? Would he use technology? How would he use that technology?

There are all kinds of opinions about this in the church today. I also have my opinions and some good reasons to support them. However, I think we miss the core issues about church leadership today when we focus on these questions. By focusing on the wrong questions, we get the wrong answers.

The core question is this: How would Jesus bring the kingdom of God to life today in your community? To this question, we can be relatively confident in our answer: he would use the same basic method he used two thousand years ago.

First, he would do most of his ministry where people live and work. He would not wait for people to come to him in a religious setting. I'm not saying we should get rid of church buildings. I'm only saying Jesus would not sit in his office for forty hours every week, running the church business. He would be out with the people.

Second, he would not be looking for ways to make the church a power structure. Jesus came to proclaim God's rule here on earth. While the disciples were longing for an overthrow of the existing rulers, Christ came to transform people and create a new society. Although Jesus healed and performed many miracles as a sign of his kingdom power, his main goal was to form a new family, the church. Jesus concentrated on developing a small group of future leaders instead of trying to rally the masses to attain power. If he were leading the church today, he would be mentoring and developing a core small group and teaching them how to live as a part of God's family.

Jesus utilized homes as a base for his own ministry and as an evangelistic strategy. He focused on the home because he knew that when families were restored into a right relationship with God, his gospel message would continue to have a lasting impact. Jesus didn't invite people to join a large crowd. He asked them to become disciples and part of his new family.

Jesus also instructed his disciples how to penetrate homes. He taught them how to reach an entire region through the establishment of a house church. He asked them to look for divine appointments (persons of peace) and to concentrate on one home, rather than going door to door. From the home base, the disciples could then reach the rest of the town or city.

What might this mean for you and your leadership team? Let me offer some positive and negative advice.

On a positive note: Establish key cell groups where Christ's peace reigns supreme. Don't quickly move from house-to-house until strong home bases are established where God has called you to minister. Don't focus on outward results that look good on paper and impress others, but shrivel up in the long term. This will take time. In fact, I'm sure it will take more time than you realize. Cell group ministry is a long-term strategy, not an instant growth technique.

On a negative note, avoid depending upon buildings or outward structures, especially when it requires you go into massive debt. Instead, focus on Christ's rule in the lives of those in your congregation and base your growth on the cell infrastructure, which should then build the quality and quantity of your celebration gathering. Just as Christ used the homes in his day as his primary base of ministry, we need to establish family-like cell groups that will bring new health and life to the family of God.

Some questions to ask:

1. Is God's kingdom rule paramount in your thinking?
2. How does Christ's strategy inform your own ministry?
3. Are you encouraging your church members to look for divine appointments?
4. Are you practicing team outreach through cell ministry?
5. Are you contemplating going into debt to purchase a church building?

TURNING THE PRIVATE HOME INTO A PUBLIC PLACE OF REDEMPTION

Chapter 5 Review:

God established the early church in the house environment which spread over the entire Roman Empire. Most house churches were between ten to twenty people, although some house churches were larger. The content of the house meetings was flexible and dynamic. They celebrated the Lord's Supper as a meal, enjoyed fellowship, ministered to one another from the Word of God, practiced hospitality, prayed, worshipped, baptized new believers, and evangelized.

The genius of the house church structure was that it changed lives where people lived and worked. People saw Christianity in living color. The early disciples lived Christ's command, "By this all people will know that you are my disciples, if you love one another" (John 13:35). It was natural for the home to be the base of operation for the early church. As we have observed, the home was the center of life for people.

I've seen people argue that the early church leaders developed a strategic plan for the house churches, and that if only we adopted that strategy today, we too would duplicate their growth and impact. On one level I agree, but on a deeper level this is much too simplistic.

Today we have private homes with security fences to keep people out. We often have small group meetings and no one knows about it except for other small group members. So how can we bridge the gap between the house church meetings in the first century and meeting in homes today?

One of the principal ways to imitate the early church success is found in the practice of hospitality. Cell ministry often fails to expand because of the lack of hospitality among church members. Instead of seeing their homes as God's possessions, people view them as their own castles.

Hospitality begins with leadership. If those with key leadership positions do not open their homes, most likely others will not either. Sharing meals with other leaders, with other group members, and with neighbors will elevate the experience of community throughout the church. It will also redeem the home and provide practical ways of making it a center for ministry.

While the home is not the only place to have a cell group—some will lead groups at work, a restaurant, or on a university campus—the home is a primary way to engage people where we live and work. People need to see their neighborhoods and work places as mission fields, planting cell groups as the main strategy.

We can also learn from the early church about the organic nature of the cell meeting. I personally like structured cell meetings, but I'm increasingly seeing the need to focus on edification as the primary goal of each cell group. In other words, it's not the lesson material that makes a great cell meeting as much as the ministry that takes place among the members. Yes, I do believe each house meeting should be based on God's Word, but edification *(oikodomeo)* should be the priority.

If you are a cell leader, make sure you listen more than talk, encourage each person to participate, and do not allow one person to dominate the entire meeting. Cell groups probe deeply into people's lives and are more like the early house churches, which were dynamic, free-flowing, and controlled by the Spirit of God. Remember to model what you want others to follow.

Some questions to ask:

1. Is your church practicing hospitality? How can you improve in this area?
2. Do you see your church as a community of house churches?
3. Is your church organic in its outlook?
4. Are you and the members of the church living out the claims of the gospel before your neighbors?

EXPANDING THROUGH CONNECTIONS

> ## Chapter 6 Review:
> *The cultural framework of the early church was the oikos structure. Oikos refers to the extended family of New Testament times, which not only included immediate relatives but also slaves, freemen, hired workers, and sometimes tenants and partners in a trade. The gospel flowed along these family lines in New Testament times. As Jesus transformed people, they behaved differently within their family relationships. Husbands cared for their wives, slaves were treated with dignity, married partners submitted to one another, and love ruled. People could see the changes up close as city life was lived out in the open, and many became followers of Jesus and his new family.*

The *oikos* teaching of Scripture helps the church understand that people are already grouped in natural relationships. These web-like relationships include family, friends, co-workers, and anyone we come in contact with on a regular basis. God uses these natural links to spread his gospel message.

Rather than relying on advertising or more parking lot space, the church needs to reemphasize the natural web of relationships of each church member. Each member should grow in his or her own *oikos* network by praying for them, serving them, and then inviting them to cell and celebration.

Ralph Neighbour has done a lot of research on the early church *oikos* structure. Bill Beckham, writing about Neighbour's research, says:

Neighbour's system builds upon three Greek words that come from the same root: *oikos, oikonomos, oikodomeo.* Tom Wolf, pastor of Church on Brady, introduced the concept of *oikos* in the New Testament to Neighbour. The teaching has become central to Neighbour's theology of the Cell Church.[200]

As Neighbour discovered, the concept of *oikos* has practical implications today. It helps us remember that those who we interact with on a continual basis are part of our *oikos* and able to readily see changes made by the gospel. After seeing the changes in our own lives, they are more ready to accept the gospel message and join the family of God.

Leaders must teach members to develop relationships with family and friends—those natural life connections. After identifying who those special *oikos* relationships are, ask your members to pray daily for their salvation and for God to work in their lives. The next step is to serve those *oikos* relationships, blessing them in word and deed.

As your church is mobilized to minister along *oikos* lines, those who come to your church or cell will already be connected to existing friendships and will be more likely to stay connected. Discipleship or "follow-up" will happen naturally because of the *oikos* connections. Your church will begin to develop natural organic links with people, which will keep them connected.

Another principle of early church evangelism was taking advantage of the urban milieu to grow and expand. Envision how cells can reach into your town or city by developing *oikos* friendships, meeting needs, prayer walking, and especially welcoming those in the area to join a cell group and participate in the family of God.

---

200 Bill Beckham, *The River* (Houston, TX: Touch Glocal, 2010), pp. 51-52.

Some questions to ask:

1. Is each cell church member developing a web of non-Christian relationships?
2. Is your church praying and then following up on those *oikos* friendships?
3. How can you improve in this area?
4. What are you doing to start cell groups in the population centers around your church?

SIMPLE LEADERSHIP

Chapter 7 Review:

Christ's apostles led the church after Pentecost, but the early church began relying on leaders developed through house church ministry. Leadership in the early church was organic, charismatic, non-hierarchical, home based, team-oriented, and promoted both males and females. The Spirit of God through his gifts allowed each member to minister. Females played an essential role in early leadership, and the focus was on the team, rather than one leader.

The early church viewed each house church member as a minister. Ministry through the gifts of the Spirit flowed naturally in the home environment, and leadership development was simple and dynamic. Leadership was based on God-given gifts, rather than hierarchy.

As the church moved beyond the first century, the growing authority of the bishop concentrated more and more power in the hands of centralized authority figures responsible for larger and larger groups of believers.[201] This can be illustrated by the way the Lord's Supper developed. The early believers celebrated the Lord's Supper as a meal, but by the second century it had become a ritual. Soon the liturgy performed by an official leader replaced the interactive communal life of those involved in house churches.

The church progressed from the family of God meeting in homes to institutionalized religion. The church turned from simplicity and grew in complexity. The authors of *Home Cell Groups and House Churches* write,

> For generations after the apostles, the church continued its spontaneous lay (people of God) witness in the cities and along the great trade routes of the empire. However, some ideological changes were taking place which were altering the New Testament theology of the church. The plurality and equality of leadership was giving way to a hierarchical arrangement with bishops becoming the central figure followed by the presbyters (who later became priests) and deacons. Later such roles as exorcists and acolytes were added. It appears that after the apostles, the bishops, who were at first pastors, assumed a role of authority as well as leadership. The bishop would have been pastor of a house church; but in time his congregation came to be the central one, and the other house congregations in a given city would then be pastored by presbyters under the authority of the bishop. In a given city, certainly in the Western church, only one pastor in a city could be a bishop.[202]

---

201 Osiek and Balch, p. 35.
202 Hadaway, DuBose, Wright, pp. 69-70.

As the years passed, the church became more and more hierarchical. Eventually Luther made a break with the structured Catholic church and established the preaching of the Word as the central place in church life. Luther helped liberate the church doctrinally, but did little in the area of ecclesiology.

Most non-Catholic churches today in the West flow out of the Protestant reformation. The duty of the professional clergy is to preach the Word on Sunday and then shepherd the flock during the week. But like the early church, we need to move people from sitting in rows on Sunday to participating actively in cell groups and then developing leadership skills in a natural, dynamic environment.

While I have no desire to criticize any specific church tradition, I do invite you to think through how your church leadership is structured. What has been the primary influence upon the way your leadership structure operates? The Bible? Church tradition? I have seen churches that wanted to develop the organic life of family and even understood how to do it. Yet, they held on to their formal traditions and the corresponding rules developed by a formal church structure. They were trying to mix oil and water.

Please consider these ideas that will help you develop a leadership process that fits this vision for simple, family church life.

Think organic. Develop leaders from within. Those who are leading cells should be those you promote to positions of overseer or elder. Those who have led and multiplied groups are the ones you want to plant future churches or send off to seminary for more training.

Think fringes. Some of the best future leaders are those who don't look anything like leaders today. They don't have all the qualities of what was expected of church leaders in the past. In other words, they are not called to "professional" ministry. They are called to be teachers, carpenters, and mothers. They lead God's people in the midst of their vocations, not because they are paid to do so, but because they feel God's inward desire and compulsion.

Think women. Allow females to participate in cell leadership and other leadership positions, just as they did in the early church. Don't bottleneck the flow of female leadership. God has freely given them the gifts of the Spirit, just as he has to the males. Your tradition might not allow this practice. If that is the case, then you will need to determine how you will address this issue. Hopefully your church will examine the practice of the early church, though I realize that some churches will not agree with my conclusions on this matter.

Think teamwork. One of the best ways to empower simple, organic leadership in your groups is to develop leadership teams of two or three people as opposed to solo leaders. Teams of leaders are far more healthy and biblical. Establish teams of leaders for your cell groups as well as your pastoral team. For example, many cell groups use the term "co-leader" or "assistant leader," but in doing so they cut themselves off to additional team members. Why not just use the term "team member" and then form a strong team of three to five people.

Think equipping. Equip people to use the gifts of the Spirit in cell groups, asking each member to identify his or her gift in the warm home atmosphere. Remember that all of the gift passages were written to house churches, and the best place to identify and use the gifts of the Spirit is the cell group. Those who faithfully and fruitfully use their gifts in the cell setting may be asked to do so in the larger celebration gatherings.

Some questions to ask:

1.   Are you developing your leaders from the cell structure?

2. Are the church overseers (e.g., elders, deacons) actually shepherding people in a cell environment?

3. Are you utilizing women in the church?

4. Are you focusing on team ministry or using the lone ranger approach to leadership?

5. Are the members encouraged to discover and use their gifts in the cell environment? How can your church improve in this area?

CELEBRATION GATHERINGS

Chapter 8 Review:

The early church primarily met in house churches, but those house churches were not independent entities. At times the house churches gathered regularly together for larger meetings, as we can see in both Jerusalem and Corinth. At other times those gatherings were less frequent. The New Testament writers used the word ecclesia to refer to the house church gatherings, the large gatherings, and the universal church.

History tells us that the foundation of the early church was the house church structure. We can also see that house churches were connected. At times those house churches met regularly together, as in the case of the Jerusalem church and in Corinth. At other times those connected house churches met less frequently in the larger gathering. Besides worshipping together and receiving the apostle's teaching, we don't know exactly what they did in those larger gatherings.

Today's church is often imbalanced toward two extremes. Some independent house churches do not acknowledge connections beyond themselves, which is not what took place in the early church. On the other hand, the majority of today's churches have become imbalanced on the Sunday celebration side. Small groups are often a programmatic technique to keep people coming back to Sunday celebration, rather than being at the very heart of ministry.

Churches must determine if they are going to view the cell group as the church and the primary care structure for members, or just another program to keep people coming back to the Sunday gathering. If the church chooses to prioritize cell ministry, those cells and cell leaders need to be equipped, coached and cared for in a cell structure that includes training, coaching, and celebrating together.

If you are the lead pastor, your principal role is to care and equip the cell leaders who in turn will care for the rest of the church. When you do gather the cells in a larger celebration gathering, see that time as a gathering of the house churches to celebrate. Mario Vega, the lead pastor of Elim, one of the largest cell churches in the world, writes,

> We only keep statistics for what takes place in cell gatherings and don't keep track of how many attend the celebration services. For Elim members, the cells are the church. The celebration is to celebrate together and enjoy the oneness of the body of Christ.[203]

Elim considers the cell meetings as the primary place of ministry, while not neglecting the importance of gathering those house groups to hear God's Word and worship the Creator.

---

203 Mario Vega wrote this on the JCG blog on March 29, 2012: http://joelcomiskey-group.com/blog_2/2012/03/29/the-balance-between-the-celebration-and-the-cell/

When this approach is taken, the larger celebration service is a time to minister to the leaders and members. Preaching focuses on expounding God's inerrant Word to make sure the leaders and members are well grounded in biblical truth. Then the teaching and preaching is reinforced in the house church setting through lessons that correlate with the preaching. For many this will prove to be a radical shift. Some might even think of it as diminishing the value of the large church services. I actually argue that this approach elevates the celebration service as people will attend not as spectators and spiritual consumers but as worshippers and participants.

This has practical implications on areas like announcements and vision casting. Announcements should focus on how your church is reaching people through the family house church strategy and to give members a vision about what the church is doing to reach new areas through house-to-house ministry. Vision casting in these celebration meetings should be geared around existing cells and envisioning new groups. If there are visitors in the larger gatherings, try to connect them to cell members who will welcome them into a new family.

Some questions to ask:

1. Are you experiencing the simplicity of the New Testament church?
2. Do you see the cell as the church?
3. Do you see the celebration service as the coming together of the home groups?
4. As lead pastor, do you have a leadership team, made up of those who are involved in cell ministry?
5. Are you involved in cell ministry?

A JOURNEY BACKWARD TO MOVE FORWARD

God is calling the church today to journey backward to apply the values and ministry practices found in the New Testament.

We must always come back to the reasons we do things. Some motivations seem urgent, but fail over time. Biblical foundations for cell ministry provide the enduring motivation that will help us persist through dry, difficult seasons. Cell ministry motivated from a biblical theology will sustain, encourage, and give new vision to the church over the long haul.

The church as God's family is a key insight from this book. The family character of Christ's church flows from God's Trinitarian nature and should influence all we do and say. People will be attracted by the love among members and will believe on Jesus as a result of that love.

God also wants the church to experience organic life in which leadership is developed in relational community. An organic church is mobilized around web-like friendships with non-believers through cell ministry. The celebration gathering of the family is a time of refreshing and fine-tuning.

Not every chapter in this book will be equally relevant to you. Perhaps your church is already family oriented and community based. You might even call your groups family cells. Perhaps you need to work on organic outreach through home ministry or simple leadership development. Or maybe you are developing leaders rapidly, but are failing to apply Christ's kingdom values in your small groups. Perhaps this book has shown you the significance of the house church. Up to this point, your celebration gatherings have been all important. God is showing you the need to scale back and refocus your priorities.

Whether you are in a small or large church, a growing or plateaued one, my prayer is that you will be encouraged to apply the insights from the New Testament church to your current situation. As you do, your church will become more biblical and fruitful and ultimately bring glory to the triune God.

RESOURCES BY JOEL COMISKEY

Joel Comiskey's previous books cover the following topics

- Leading a cell group (*How to Lead a Great Cell Group Meeting,* 2001, 2009).

- How to multiply the cell group (*Home Cell Group Explosion,* 1998).

- How to prepare spiritually for cell ministry (*An Appointment with the King,* 2002, 2011).

- How to practically organize your cell system (*Reap the Harvest,*1999; *Cell Church Explosion,* 2004).

- How to train future cell leaders (*Leadership Explosion,* 2001; *Live,* 2007; *Encounter,* 2007; *Grow,* 2007; *Share,* 2007; *Lead,* 2007; *Coach,* 2008; *Discover,* 2008).

- How to coach/care for cell leaders (*How to be a Great Cell Group Coach,* 2003; *Groups of Twelve,* 2000; *From Twelve to Three,* 2002).

- How the gifts of the Spirit work within the cell group (*The Spirit-filled Small Group,* 2005, 2009; *Discover,* 2008).

- How to fine tune your cell system (*Making Cell Groups Work Navigation Guide,* 2003).

- Principles from the second largest church in the world (*Passion and Persistence,* 2004).

- How cell church works in North America (*The Church that Multiplies,* 2007, 2009).

- How to plant a church (*Planting Churches that Reproduce,* 2009)

- How to be a relational disciple (*Relational Disciple,* 2010).

- How to distinguish truth and myths *(Myths and Truths of the Cell Church,* 2011).

All of the books listed are available from *Joel Comiskey Group* **by**

How To Lead A Great Cell Group Meeting: So People Want to Come Back

 Do people expectantly return to your group meetings every week? Do you have fun and experience joy during your meetings? Is everyone participating in discussion and ministry? You can lead a great cell group meeting, one that is life changing and dynamic. Most people don't realize that they can create a God-filled atmosphere because they don't know how. Now the secret is out. This guide will show you how to:

- Prepare yourself spiritually to hear God during the meeting
- Structure the meeting so it flows
- Spur people in the group to participate and share their lives openly
- Share your life with others in the group
- Create stimulating questions
- Listen effectively to discover what is transpiring in others' lives
- Encourage and edify group members
- Open the group to non-Christians
- See the details that create a warm atmosphere

By implementing these time-tested ideas, your group meetings will become the hot-item of your members' week. They will go home wanting more and return each week bringing new people with them. 140 pgs.

Home Cell Group Explosion: How Your Small Group Can Grow and Multiply

  The book crystallizes the author's findings in some eighteen areas of research, based on a meticulous questionnaire that he submitted to cell church leaders in eight countries around the world, locations that he also visited personally for his research. The detailed notes in the back of the book offer the student of cell church growth a rich mine for further reading. The beauty of Comiskey's book is that he not only summarizes his survey results in a thoroughly convincing way but goes on to analyze in practical ways many of his survey results in separate chapters. The happy result is that any cell church leader, intern or member completing this quick read will have his priorities/values clearly aligned and ready to be followed-up. If you are a pastor or small group leader, you should devour this book! It will encourage you and give you simple, practical steps for dynamic small group life and growth. 175 pgs.

An Appointment with the King: *Ideas for Jump-Starting Your Devotional Life*

With full calendars and long lists of things to do, people often put on hold life's most important goal: building an intimate relationship with God. Often, believers wish to pursue the goal but are not sure how to do it. They feel frustrated or guilty when their attempts at personal devotions seem empty and unfruitful. With warm, encouraging writing, Joel Comiskey guides readers on how to set a daily appointment with the King and make it an exciting time they will look forward to. This book first answers the question "Where do I start?" with step-by-step instructions on how to spend time with God and practical ideas for experiencing him more fully. Second, it highlights the benefits of spending time with God, including joy, victory over sin, and spiritual guidance. The book will help Christians tap into God's resources on a daily basis, so that even in the midst of busyness they can walk with him in intimacy and abundance. 175 pgs.

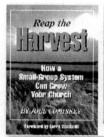

Reap the Harvest: *How a Small Group System Can Grow Your Church*

Have you tried small groups and hit a brick wall? Have you wondered why your groups are not producing the fruit that was promised? Are you looking to make your small groups more effective? Cell-church specialist and pastor Dr. Joel Comiskey studied the world's most successful cell churches to determine why they grow. The key: They have embraced specific principles. Conversely, churches that do not embrace these same principles have problems with their groups and therefore do not grow. Cell churches are successful not because they have small groups but because they can support the groups. In this book, you will discover how these systems work. 236 pgs.

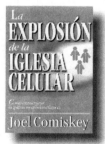

La Explosión de la Iglesia Celular: *Cómo Estructurar la Iglesia en Células Eficaces* (Editorial Clie, 2004)

This book is only available in Spanish and contains Joel Comiskey's research of eight of the world's largest cell churches, five of which reside in Latin America. It details how to make the transition from a traditional church to the cell church structure and many other valuable insights, including: the history of the cell church, how to organize your church to become a praying church, the most important principles of the cell church, and how to raise up an army of cell leaders. 236 pgs.

Leadership Explosion: *Multiplying Cell Group Leaders to Reap the Harvest*

Some have said that cell groups are leader breeders. Yet even the best cell groups often have a leadership shortage. This shortage impedes growth and much of the harvest goes untouched. Joel Comiskey has discovered why some churches are better at raising up new cell leaders than others. These churches do more than pray and hope for new leaders. They have an intentional strategy, a plan that will quickly equip as many new leaders as possible. In this book, you will discover the training models these churches use to multiply leaders. You will discover the underlying principles of these models so that you can apply them. 202 pgs.

FIVE-BOOK EQUIPPING SERIES

#1: Live   #2: Encounter   #3: Grow   #4: Share   #5: Lead

The five book equipping series is designed to train a new believer all the way to leading his or her own cell group. Each of the five books contains eight lessons. Each lesson has interactive activities that helps the trainee reflect on the lesson in a personal, practical way.

Live starts the training by covering key Christian doctrines, including baptism and the Lord's supper. 85 pgs.

Encounter guides the believer to receive freedom from sinful bondages. The Encounter book can be used one-on-one or in a group. 91 pgs.

Grow gives step-by-step instruction for having a daily quiet time, so that the believer will be able to feed him or herself through spending daily time with God. 87 pgs.

Share instructs the believer how to communicate the gospel message in a winsome, personal way. This book also has two chapters on small group evangelism. 91 pgs.

Lead prepares the Christian on how to facilitate an effective cell group. This book would be great for those who form part of a small group team. 91 pgs.

TWO-BOOK ADVANCED TRAINING SERIES

COACH   DISCOVER

Coach and Discover make-up the Advanced Training, prepared specifically to take a believer to the next level of maturity in Christ.

Coach prepares a believer to coach another cell leader. Those experienced in cell ministry often lack understanding on how to coach someone else. This book provides step-by-step instruction on how to coach a new cell leader from the first meeting all the way to giving birth to a new group. The book is divided into eight lessons, which are interactive and help the potential coach deal with real-life, practical coaching issues. 85 pgs.

Discover clarifies the twenty gifts of the Spirit mentioned in the New Testament. The second part shows the believer how to find and use his or her particular gift. This book is excellent to equip cell leaders to discover the giftedness of each member in the group. 91 pgs.

How to be a Great Cell Group Coach:
Practical insight for Supporting and Mentoring Cell Group Leaders

Research has proven that the greatest contributor to cell group success is the quality of coaching provided for cell group leaders. Many are serving in the position of a coach, but they don't fully understand what they are supposed to do in this position. Joel Comiskey has identified seven habits of great cell group coaches. These include: Receiving from God, Listening to the needs of the cell group leader, Encouraging the cell group leader, Caring for the multiple aspects of a leader's life, Developing the cell leader in various aspects of leadership, Strategizing with the cell leader to create a plan, Challenging the cell leader to grow.

Practical insights on how to develop these seven habits are outlined in section one. Section two addresses how to polish your skills as a coach with instructions on diagnosing problems in a cell group, how to lead coaching meetings, and what to do when visiting a cell group meeting. This book will prepare you to be a great cell group coach, one who mentors, supports, and guides cell group leaders into great ministry. 139 pgs.

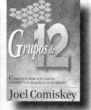

Groups of Twelve: *A New Way to Mobilize Leaders and Multiply Groups in Your Church*

This book clears the confusion about the Groups of 12 model. Joel dug deeply into the International Charismatic Mission in Bogota, Colombia and other G12 churches to learn the simple principles that G12 has to offer your church. This book also contrasts the G12 model with the classic 5x5 and shows you what to do with this new model of ministry. Through onsite research, international case studies, and practical experience, Joel Comiskey outlines the G12 principles that your church can use today.

Billy Hornsby, director of the Association of Related Churches, says, "Joel Comiskey shares insights as a leader who has himself raised up numerous leaders. From how to recognize potential leaders to cell leader training to time-tested principles of leadership-this book has it all. The accurate comparisons of various training models make it a great resource for those who desire more leaders. Great book!" 182 pgs.

From Twelve To Three: *How to Apply G12 Principles in Your Church*

The concept of the Groups of 12 began in Bogota, Colombia, but now it is sweeping the globe. Joel Comiskey has spent years researching the G12 structure and the principles behind it.

From his experience as a pastor, trainer, and consultant, he has discovered that there are two ways to embrace the G12 concept: adopting the entire model or applying the principles that support the model.

This book focuses on the application of principles rather than adoption of the entire model. It outlines the principles and provides a modified application which Joel calls the G12.3. This approach presents a pattern that is adaptable to many different church contexts.

The concluding section illustrates how to implement the G12.3 in various kinds of churches, including church plants, small churches, large churches, and churches that already have cells. 178 pgs.

The Spirit-filled Small Group: *Leading Your Group to Experience the Spiritual Gifts.* The focus in many of today's small groups has shifted from Spirit-led transformation to just another teacher-student Bible study. But exercising every member's spiritual gifts is vital to the effectiveness of the group. With insight born of experience in more than twenty years of small group ministry, Joel Comiskey explains how leaders and participants alike can be supernaturally equipped to deal with real-life issues. Put these principles into practice and your small group will never be the same!

This book works well with Comiskey's training book, **Discover.** It fleshes out many of the principles in Comiskey's training book. Chuck Crismier, radio host, Viewpoint, writes, "Joel Comiskey has again provided the Body of Christ with an important tool to see God's Kingdom revealed in and through small groups." 191 pgs.

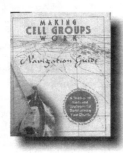

Making Cell Groups Work Navigation Guide: *A Toolbox of Ideas and Strategies for Transforming Your Church.* For the first time, experts in cell group ministry have come together to provide you with a 600 page reference tool like no other. When Ralph Neighbour, Bill Beckham, Joel Comiskey and Randall Neighbour compiled new articles and information under careful orchestration and in-depth understanding that Scott Boren brings to the table, it's as powerful as private consulting! Joel Comiskey has an entire book within this mammoth 600 page work. There are also four additional authors.

Passion and Persistence: *How the Elim Church's Cell Groups Penetrated an Entire City for Jesus*

This book describes how the Elim Church in San Salvador grew from a small group to 116,000 people in 10,000 cell groups. Comiskey takes the principles from Elim and applies them to churches in North   America and all over the world. Ralph Neighbour says: "I believe this book will be remember as one of the most important ever written about a cell church movement! I experienced the *passion* when visiting Elim many years ago. Comiskey's report about Elim is not a *pattern* to be slavishly copied. It is a journey into grasping the true theology and methodology of the New Testament church. You'll discover how the Elim Church fans into flame their passion for Jesus and His Word, how they organize their cells to penetrate a city and world for Jesus, and how they persist until God brings the fruit." 158 pgs.

The Church that Multiplies: *Growing a Healthy Cell Church in North America*

Does the cell church strategy work in North America? We hear about exciting cell churches in Colombia and Korea, but where are the dynamic North American cell churches? This book not only declares that the cell church concept does work in North America but dedicates an entire chapter to examining North American churches that are successfully using the cell strategy to grow in quality and quantity. This book provides the latest statistical research about the North American church and explains why the cell church approach restores health and growth to the church today. More than anything else, this book will provide practical solutions for pastors and lay leaders to use in implementing cell-based ministry. 181 pgs.

Planting Churches that Reproduce: *Planting a Network of Simple Churchces*

What is the best way to plant churches in the 21st century? Comiskey believes that simple, reproducible church planting is most effective. The key is to plant churches that are simple enough to grow into a movement of churches. Comiskey has been gathering material for this book for the past fifteen Years. He has also planted three churches in a wide variety of settings. Planting Churches that Reproduce is the fruit of his research and personal experience. Comiskey uses the latest North American church planting statistics, but extends the illustrations to include worldwide church planting. More than anything else, this book will provide practical solutions for those planting churches today. Comiskey's book is a must-read book for all those interested in establishing Christ-honoring, multiplying churches. 176 pgs.

The Relational Disciple: *How God Uses Community to Shape Followers of Jesus*

Jesus lived with His disciples for three years and taught them life lessons as a group. After three years, he commanded them to "go and do likewise" (Matthew 28:18-20). Jesus discipled His followers through relationships—and He wants us to do the same. Scripture is full of exhortations to love and serve one another. This book will show you how. The isolation present in the western world is creating a hunger for community and the world is longing to see relational disciples in action. This book will encourage Christ-followers to allow God to use the natural relationships in life—family, friends, work relationships, cells, church, and missions to mold them into relational disciples.

You Can Coach: *How to Help Leaders Build Healthy Churches through Coaching*

We've entitled this book "You Can Coach" because we believe that coaching is more about passing on what you've lived and holding others accountable in the process. Coaching doesn't require a higher degree, special talent, unique personality, or a particular spiritual gift. We believe, in fact, that God wants coaching to become a movement. We long to see the day in which every pastor has a coach and in turn is coaching someone else. In this book, you'll hear three coaches who have successfully coached pastors for many years. They will share their history, dreams, principles, and what God is doing through coaching. Our hope is that you'll be both inspired and resourced to continue your own coaching ministry in the years to come.

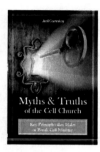

Myths & Truths of the Cell Church: *Key Principles that Make or Break Cell Ministry*

Most of the modern day cell church movement is dynamic, positive, and applicable. As is true in most endeavors, errors and false assumptions have also cropped up to destroy an otherwise healthy movement. Sometimes these false concepts caused the church to go astray completely. At other times, they led the pastor and church down a dead-end road of fruitless ministry. Regardless of how the myths were generated, they had a chilling effect on the church's ministry. In this book, Joel Comiskey tackles these errors and false assumptions, helping pastors and leaders to untangle the webs of legalism that has crept into the cell church movement. Joel then guides the readers to apply biblical, time-tested principles that will guide them into fruitful cell ministry. Each chapter begins with a unique twist. Well-known worldwide cell church leaders open each chapter by answering questions to the chapter's topic in the form of an email dialogue. Whether you're starting out for the first time in cell ministry or a seasoned veteran, this book will give you the tools to help your ministry stay fresh and fruitful.e.

INDEX